"*Named by God* will capture your heart, mess with your mind, and loudly declare, 'Redemption rocks!' Kasey Van Norman reveals her deepest wounds, asks hard questions, and points readers to grace-filled hope. Buy a copy for yourself and ten to give away. I love this book!"

CAROL KENT, speaker and author of *Between a Rock and a Grace Place* and *When I Lay My Isaac Down*

"You are named and called by God to worship him with your life: the good, the bad, and the ugly. Throughout the honest and raw pages of *Named by God*, Kasey Van Norman reveals how she worshiped God despite some dark and desperate years. Her story will bring hope to anyone struggling with their faith because it so wonderfully reminds us all that we are named by God."

SCOTT LINDSEY, ministry relations director for Logos Bible Software

"In *Named by God*, Kasey candidly reveals how to reach the struggling and disheartened. She sets the events of her own past in the context of Christ's redemptive work while gently encouraging readers to do the same. Through her testimony and through Scripture, she reminds us that we aren't defined by our failures—or even our successes. We are named by God, and we find our identity in Christ."

REBECCA KRUYSWIJK, managing editor of *Bible Study Magazine*

named by God

overcoming your past,
transforming your present,
embracing your future

kasey van norman

TYNDALE HOUSE PUBLISHERS, INC.
CAROL STREAM, ILLINOIS

Visit Tyndale online at www.tyndale.com.

Visit Kasey Van Norman's website at www.kaseyvannorman.com.

TYNDALE and Tyndale's quill logo are registered trademarks of Tyndale House Publishers, Inc.

Named by God: Overcoming Your Past, Transforming Your Present, Embracing Your Future

Designed by Daniel Farrell

Edited by Stephanie Rische

Published in association with literary agent Jenni Burke of D. C. Jacobson and Associates, an author management company, www.DCJacobson.com.

Library of Congress Cataloging-in-Publication Data

Van Norman, Kasey.
  Named by God : overcoming your past, transforming your present, embracing your future /
Kasey Van Norman.
    p. cm.
    ISBN 978-1-4143-6474-2 (sc)
1. Van Norman, Kasey.   2. Christian biography.   3. Suffering—Religious aspects Christianity.
I. Title.
  BR1725.V24A3 2012
  277.3'083092—dc23
  [B]   2011044281

Printed in the United States of America

18 17 16 15 14 13 12

7   6   5   4   3   2   1

To Jesus Christ—the lover of my soul, the only one who sees my heart as it truly is. If nothing else, may these words bring you glory and honor. I praise you for granting these words to me, one of the most undeserving of your children. You are my life, my joy, and my daily pursuit. You are my heartbeat and the song that I sing. Thank you for the adventure and privilege of life. And thank you for loving the broken ones.

Contents

Introduction

*Through him God created everything in the heavenly realms
and on earth. He made the things we can see and the things we
can't see—such as thrones, kingdoms, rulers, and authorities
in the unseen world. Everything was created through him
and for him. He existed before anything else, and he holds
all creation together.* COLOSSIANS 1:16-17

I OFTEN WONDER WHY it took me so long to get it. As a child
practically born in the church nursery and then raised in the Bible
Belt, how did I reach my late twenties as one of the most insecure,
self-defeated, guilt-ridden individuals on the face of the earth?
How is it that this devoted Christian girl from East Texas who
sang in the church choir and led small-group Bible study suddenly
found herself tossing back a bottleful of Xanax to end it all?

As a believer from the age of nine, I found it easy to live my
life accepting that Jesus was my *Savior*. I mean, who doesn't want
to be saved from their stupid mistakes, from their moral failures
and compromises, and—best of all—from death and the grave? I
imagine many of you can relate. We may not even be conscious of
it, but soon enough we're coasting through life with Jesus as our
"step-in Savior"—believing in him only when we're aware there is
something to be saved from. But sooner or later, we inevitably find
ourselves at a crossroads. That's precisely what happened to me.

After a couple of decades of splashing in the shallow end of
Christianity, I became plagued by questions that seemed to have
no answers. I got bombarded by doubts about who I was and why
I existed. At some point, looking within myself for the answer was

no longer enough. And simply buying into God as my Savior was no longer enough either.

If you haven't already noticed from the cover of the book, I have a tattoo that wraps around my left wrist. I should pause here to note that Christians have different opinions about the morality of tattoos, and I'm okay with that. But that's not really the issue I want to get into now. I'd rather share with you the meaning behind my tattoo, because it's not just there for looks. It holds spiritual significance for me.

The most obvious element of a tattoo is that it is permanent. Just as the ink is forever cut into the flesh of my wrist, as a believer in Jesus Christ, I am also permanently marked with his redemption.

My tattoo says, "Redeemed," and that's not something I chose lightly. I simply couldn't think of a more appropriate and powerful word to look at on a daily basis. It is the one common denominator of my life that I need to be reminded of most often—that I have been redeemed by God, despite my past sin or future failings. Take a moment to bask in the biblical definitions of the word *redeem*: "to free from what distresses or harms; to free from captivity by payment of ransom; to free from the consequences of sin."

My greatest internal struggle over the years has not been to love the Lord but to believe that he loves me back! The word *redeemed* on my wrist reminds me that despite my sin and failures, despite my unworthiness, despite my lack of faithfulness, the Lord remains faithful to love me and pursue me. Galatians 3:13-14 puts it this way: "Christ *redeemed* us from the curse of the law by becoming a curse for us, for it is written: 'Cursed is everyone who is hung on a pole.' He *redeemed* us in order that the blessing given to Abraham might come to the Gentiles through Christ Jesus, so that by faith we might receive the promise of the Spirit" (NIV, emphasis added).

When you make the choice to live a redeemed life, you will never spend another breath in the bondage of guilt, shame, and regret over your yesterdays. You will no longer live as one oppressed by the enemy and his sinful schemes. You will no longer fear death, for you will truly believe that the one who is in you is more powerful than the clutches of the grave.

If you were to see my tattoo in person, you would notice that the artistic detail of the cuff wraps all the way around my wrist, with no beginning and no end. To me it represents my captivity to Christ—that I desire forever, with no beginning or end, to be in a state of surrender to my King and my Lord. It is a visible reminder that I belong to Christ—that I have been named by him.

So what does it mean to be named by God? In one sense, merely to be a human existing on this earth is to be stamped with God's imprint, since we were all created in his image from the beginning (see Genesis 1:27). Whether we choose to acknowledge God as our Creator or not, we are all born with a "God code"— a strand of spiritual DNA that hardwires us to know and serve a power higher than ourselves. However, *being born* as one named by God and *living* as one named by God are two different roads.

To be named by God—and to live that way—is to abide in a constant state of redemption and surrender. It is a place of knowing who you are in Christ and knowing that your true identity is found in him. It is a place of recognizing that other people's opinions and attitudes toward you no longer dictate your worth. It is a place where religion and rules fade away and your connection with your Creator becomes all the more central. And it is a place where your every word, every thought, every action is preceded by a clear move of the Lord. Being named by God is finding yourself by losing yourself—redemption and surrender.

Shallow-Water Savior

Surrender is the only way to freedom, but it can be terrifying. We can't just dip our toes in; we have to dive in headfirst. When I was a young woman, just eighteen years old, I found myself standing at the edge of surrender. I knew quite a bit about being a Christian, because I had felt the disgust for myself and my sin for many years. I certainly knew how to look like a Christian—show up at church, wear a fashionable dress, carry a Bible, quote a Scripture verse from time to time, hang out with Christian friends, serve in a ministry, and maybe even join a Bible study when I felt others might be catching on to who I really was outside the pristine, stained-glass sanctuary.

I had splashed in the shallows of God, had felt the refreshing spray of the ocean caress my ankles, but I'd never made it out to the depths. I could hear the deep water calling to me, inviting me to a life of adventure and joy, and I longed for it to envelop me completely. It was only steps in front of me, and yet there I stood, frozen in fear. I longed for the beauty and power of the waves and surf, but I was terrified of that unknown force that offers no guarantee of ease for those who choose to embrace the waves.

But every time I gathered my courage and poised my muscles to dive into the depths of God, scenes flooded through my mind in full color and sound—that one-night stand; the evenings of drunken stupor just to void myself of emotion; that lie that destroyed those closest to me; the rumor about me that turned out to be true; all the times I failed myself, others, and God. I was sure I had disqualified myself from God's grace and blessing on my life.

I write this book, dear reader, because I lived in the shallow water far too long. I have experienced the exhilarating freedom of diving into the depths with God, and I want to invite you on this adventure too. I write this book for *you*, oh treasured one of the King.

I write this book so that you may no longer simply desire to be free, but that you may feel freedom seep from the very pores of your skin. I write this book so that you may no longer only talk of a life filled with hope and peace, but that you may begin to breathe it in and out on a moment-by-moment basis. I write this book so that you will not live one more day as a victim of circumstances or other people, but as a victor! I write this book with a prayer that, as I strip away my own masks and confess my sinful rebellion (yes, even as a Christian), it might ignite a passion deep within your soul for your Creator. I write this book so that you might see for yourself what authentic transformation and abundant living look like—that you will no longer wade complacently in the shallow end with your Savior, but that you will jump wholeheartedly into the deep end with your Lord.

The Highway of Your Past, Present, and Future

With each birthday, we change. With each death, we change. With each great love and each bitter heartbreak, we change. With each hurtful word and each cut of betrayal, we change. With each burst of happiness and each tear-inducing laugh, we change. With each good story, great friendship, and meaningful conversation, we change.

Our lives are in a constant state of change, moving fluidly between the past, the present, and the future. And so it is until the day we die. We can't stop change or do much to control it, but we can control the way we react to what happens to us along the way. With God's help, we can overcome our past, transform our present, and embrace our future.

On this highway of learning to live as one named by God, our journey will unfold in three parts. First, we will go down the winding road of our pasts, investigating the potholes of family baggage and original sin and how they impact the way we view ourselves and others. Much like a journey on a long stretch of road, we cannot know where we are going until we know where we've been. I have wasted loads of sideways energy fueling the desire to forget what has happened in my past. Somewhere along the way we have been tricked into believing that if we can simply ignore what has happened to us, it will lose its hold on us. The truth is, however, that God does not intend for us to forget our past because it has the potential to make us stronger, more purpose-filled people. God can redeem those experiences and use them to transform us into a more accurate image of his Son. The key is that we must let him into those places so that we can see him—and ourselves—more clearly.

Next, we will hit the rest stop of our present. There we will unpack our tendency to lose our focus on God's calling for our lives. It's easy to get so hung up in either the past or the future that we fail to live fully in the present. We bring mountains of anxiety and fear on ourselves when we focus on the phases of our lives that no longer exist or do not yet exist. God has a calling for us to embrace right now, today.

Finally, we will feel the brisk wind of our future streaming across our faces as we catch God's vision for us. The almighty God has bigger plans than we can fathom, and he invites us to take part and join him in that adventure. Here we will learn to develop the audacious faith to be change makers in our world through the supernatural outpouring of the Holy Spirit.

—*Kasey Van Norman*

Part 1

Overcoming Your Past

LATER IN THIS BOOK we will discuss at length the incomprehensible beauty of life after Christ's grace has filled your lungs. But for now, we are going to take a brief look back. Let's get a glimpse into you—who you are, why you do the things you do, why you say the things you say, why you surround yourself with the people you do. We're going to take a trip down the beautiful (or ugly) highway of your past.

For some of us, this is very rocky terrain. It's not a place we want anyone in our lives to visit and not a place we particularly desire to spend much time in either. In fact, as far as our map of life goes, we may have tried to erase the roads that brought us suffering and pain, the roads with potholes that resulted in serious damage, and the roads from childhood that may still be under major construction.

If you are tempted to stop reading or skip to the next section at this point, please pay attention to the flashing lights and wait, because I am going to make a deal with you, my friend. I will not ask you to go down any unsteady path I haven't been willing to go down myself. I, too, have traveled my share of dangerous roads—some of them dead ends. And at times I kept on driving, only to find myself barely hanging on at the edge of a cliff.

So let's do this together, shall we? You're in the driver's seat, and I'm right next to you on the passenger's side. Grip the steering wheel tight—until your knuckles turn white, if necessary! (By the way, the steering wheel for this trip is whatever good, sturdy Bible you've got handy, and our tour guide is none other than the Creator of the universe.) It may be a bumpy and curvy ride for you, but he has been down this road many times before. Take comfort knowing that he's the one who made this road in the first place—and he made you, too. "In him we were also chosen, having been predestined according to the plan of him who works out everything in conformity with the purpose of his will" (Ephesians 1:11, NIV).

CHAPTER 1

Family Ties

ANYONE WHO HAS SPENT ANY TIME as the passenger while I'm driving will be quick to tell you that I am horrible with directions. In fact, it makes me crazy that my husband, Justin, has this sixth sense when it comes to where we are and where we're going. He can simply "feel" that we need to turn east or west, and what really gets me is that he's almost always right. The truth is, I'm jealous. I want to be able to just sense which direction is right without having to look at a map. And by the time my tearful ramblings force me to pull over and unfold the thing, it is not a pretty sight. By that time I am in such a pride-induced fit of bitterness that I am actually resentful toward the piece of paper. (Yeah, I know, real mature.)

What I find even more troubling, though, is the similar tendency I have when I lose my sense of direction in life. I'm embarrassed to admit that sometimes I'd rather drive for miles in the wrong direction than be told I'm lost and in need of directions. That's because I know that the moment I unfold my map, I'll be forced to acknowledge just how far I've veered off course.

God has given us a map for our lives—a way to make sense of where we've been, where we are now, and where we're going. That map is our past.

For some of us, it makes sense that our past can serve to lead the way. Our past is rich and bright. We delight in it and praise God for it. But for others of us, that sounds like a daunting, if not ludicrous, prospect. We might want to run from our past, ignore it, build a wall around it, or burn it . . . but let it be our guide? How could that be possible with such a rocky backstory? Like it or not, however, our past will always be attached to us, just like our shadow. Whether you are an embracer or a runner when it comes to your past, you cannot escape the footsteps that bind you to those who went before you.

> Who you are right this minute has everything to do with who you were days, weeks, months, and even years ago.

Whether thoughts of your past make you want to smile or break out in hives, your past is a defining characteristic of who you are. At this point many are quick to rebut, "I am not defined by my past! I am no longer involved in those thoughts, that environment, those actions. Therefore, I cannot possibly be defined by where I have been."

But what if I told you that being defined by your past does not have to be a bad or scary thing? What if I told you that who you are right this minute has everything to do with who you were days, weeks, months, and even years ago? What would it be like to shatter all our presumptions that the past is some nightmare we are always trying to wake up from and instead embrace the footprints we have left behind (even the muddy ones)? The psalmist expresses this idea beautifully: "My suffering was good for me, for it taught me to pay attention to your decrees" (Psalm 119:71).

Child of God, when you can choose to see your past, present, and future through the filter of Christ, this rocky, winding, pothole-filled road will soon become clear, straight, and paved. Throughout part 1, we are going to dig into God's Word to see the road signs he has been showing us all along the way. We will also be able to see how he can make a beautiful journey of redemption out of even the pitfalls of our past.

Where My Story Begins

My upbringing was pretty normal, I suppose, although who really knows what "normal" is? It certainly wasn't a perfect childhood, but I do have many happy memories. My mother, who worked full-time at the local bank, was as devoted to us as she could be amid debt, laundry, dishes, and the slew of extracurricular activities my brother and sister and I were involved in. My father, who worked for the local electric company, was in and out of our home for much of my childhood. When he was around, he often found his happy place in the garage or at the hunting lease.

With my parents busy with jobs, paying the bills each month, and getting food on the table, we spent ample time with our grandparents. My grandparents were, to my best recollection, the first voices of wisdom I heard in the way of spiritual guidance. On a regular basis one of us would whine, "Gran, I *want* . . ." something or other, and like clockwork, she would lovingly respond, "We should not *want* for anything. The Lord has provided all we need. What is it you would *like* to have?"

I grew up in a small town in East Texas. And while being raised in the Bible Belt of the nation certainly had its perks, such as a church on every corner and an openness to talking about faith, below the surface of the shiny steeples and the majestic pine trees lay the most destructive force known to well-meaning Christ followers: complacency.

Church traditions and rituals had deep roots in the soil of my community. Even from an early age, I fell victim to living a life that looked religious from the outside but lacked substance. With so many self-professed Christians in the area, my biggest concern was going to church—and looking the part. Sunday mornings were bittersweet for me because I was constantly striving for perfection but never seemed to have the right outfit to be deemed worthy of mingling with the cool kids. And my parents' SUV was never new enough to park alongside the wealthier vehicles of our fellow churchgoers.

Each Sunday was the same. First a welcome and some hymns, a special solo, then the sermon (always consisting of a five-letter acrostic), and at last the invitation. I can still hear the booming voice of the well-dressed pastor as he rang out the rote call, almost songlike: "If you have yet to surrender yourself to the Holy Spirit and accept Jesus Christ as your personal Lord and Savior, please come to the front and allow me the privilege of leading you in the sinner's prayer."

I am sure that every time he spoke it, he meant it from his heart. Yet to my knowledge, no one ever came. And from what

I could tell, no one really cared that no one ever came. Myself included.

Throughout my youth, I believed religion fit into one neat box: "If you're good enough, you'll get to heaven." I knew well the stories of Noah and the Flood, David and Goliath, and the baby Jesus in the manger (mostly due to the small felt cutouts of these characters we directed during our yearly vacation Bible school sessions). But even with the Bible stories and altar calls, somehow I never grasped the true message of what it means to follow Christ. I vividly remember feeling safe, loved, and comfortable within my church bubble as a child. However, with the teenage years just around the corner and a family system quickly fraying around the edges, my cozy bubble was about to burst.

Adolescence brought many changes for me. My father and I were never particularly close, but as I grew into a young woman, we drifted further and further apart. I'm certain that our shared stubbornness had much to do with it. I was a headstrong, independent girl who desperately wanted to know her father loved her, but I was afraid that to ask would show weakness. My dad was a work-driven father who desperately wanted to tell his daughter he loved her, but he was afraid that to say so would show weakness.

My parents' inevitable divorce became final not long after my thirteenth birthday. I commemorated the event by running away from home. I see now that it was a dramatic plea for attention, but at the time, I knew of no other way to cope with the overwhelming sense of loss, doubt, and fear. From my limited teenage perspective, I somehow felt responsible for causing such devastation for my family.

Things Were Not Okay

The five years that followed ushered in one of the most rebellious, pain-filled seasons of my life. I was weak, unsure, and a prime target for the attacks of Satan. After the divorce, my parents seemed to turn into different people overnight. Both of them were racked with guilt from their decision and overtaken with fear of what was to become of our family. I suppose it was their defense mechanism, but for years they were cold and calloused, locking in all their emotions. There was no more laughing, no more crying, no more yelling—just nothing. Every waking moment seemed painful.

At the young age of thirteen I learned the ropes of "mommyhood." While my friends were going to the movies and getting their first kisses, I was reading bedtime stories, preparing meals, and spending almost every weekend taking care of my two younger siblings. With a desperate desire to fit in, I convinced myself that if I looked normal, people would treat me as such. Therefore, I quickly put together a mask of what I considered "normal." I wore it to school, to church, with my friends—pretty much all the time.

Each night, amid sobs and questions, I would tell myself that the Lord was with me and that it would be okay. But I knew down deep that things were *not* okay.

Until I was fifteen, I really held it together. In fact, I even surprised myself with what a good girl I was. I didn't go to parties, I never touched alcohol or kissed boys, and I went to church with my grandparents even when no one else in my family would go. I made the honor roll every year, and I devoted myself to my passions—music and theater—as a welcome escape from the shambles of my home life.

My first boyfriend came as a bit of a shock to me. In fact, when he asked me out for the first time, I thought it was some cruel joke. He was "Mr. Everything" at my high school, and I was "Miss Nobody"—just a freshman standing in awe of his "seniorness." In some strange way, I thought this guy was a reward from God for my being a good girl when things got bad, for taking care of my siblings when I would rather have been somewhere else, and for putting up with so much mess that I didn't deserve.

Only a few weeks into our so-called relationship, this boyfriend who claimed he didn't want to kiss until the altar raped me. It was devastating. And the pain didn't stop that day. That wound left scars on my soul that I thought would never heal. I built a protective shell around myself just to make it through each day. But on the inside, the shame I felt kept festering.

One of the most crushing blows from this experience was the effect it had on my faith. Since the moment I entered into a relationship with Jesus Christ at the age of nine, I had sensed his presence. I may not have understood what it meant to follow him completely, and he may have felt far away at times after my parents' divorce, but I had always felt that God was there.

But in that one awful moment, I was stripped of every security and comfort I had managed to hang on to. Suddenly it was as if everything I had believed about God was nothing more than a fairy tale—just a nice story to calm us down and get us to sleep at night. In the moments that followed the rape, I felt completely and utterly alone, as if a great chasm now separated me from the God I had known. I felt sure that God had grown weary of me and had tossed me aside like a piece of garbage. With every day that passed and with every breath I drew, I felt more alone, more broken, and more abandoned by God. My initial questions for

God turned into bitterness, and that bitterness eventually made my heart cold and numb.

With a sense of unworthiness in my heart, and feeling much like a used car, I went in search of love—in all the wrong places, as the old Johnny Lee hit so accurately puts it. The next five years were a blur of pain and insecurity as I engaged in numerous promiscuous relationships, was hospitalized for a severe eating disorder, and was placed in therapy for cutting myself.

The crazy thing about all this was that no one in my life really knew what kind of pain I was experiencing. I had been involved in theater from a very young age, and it turns out I had become quite a good actress. On the outside I wore my dazzling Christian mask, but it was only covering up terrified screams for help. I would leave every sexual encounter in sobs, begging God to help me find satisfaction in him and not in a boy. I would be in the middle of slashing my forearm while at the same time praying for God to make the pain go away.

An Honest Assessment

If you had asked me several years ago to tell my family history, it would have been too overshadowed with bitterness and rage to be accurate. I would have made it clear to you that it was my background—growing up without a father figure, watching my parents go through a messy divorce, and being raped as a teenager—that was responsible for all my bad decisions. I would have told you that those experiences were solely to blame for the open wound of bondage that kept oozing for years afterward. I would have said it was inevitable, after being a victim of such sin, that I would one day lash out in rebellion against God and others. But that was then. . . .

Now, after a few therapy sessions, an emotional breakdown that almost cost me my life, and a monumental move of the Holy Spirit, I have matured enough to see my family through the filtered lens of Christ, not merely with human eyes. This is a gift I pray that you, too, will receive over the course of the coming chapters.

You see, as long as I continued to view my life from a reactive point of view—"They did this to me, and as a result, I did that"— I was still making the story about *me* . . . and completely missing God! It's true that human beings make sinful choices that impact the lives of those around them. But that doesn't have to be the end of our story.

Not long ago my eyes were opened to another angle of my story. Although it's true that harmful things were done to me, I *chose* to live under this shadow. No family member chose it for me or forced me to live under that curse. Dear reader, in order for us to make a fair and healthy assessment of where we are now in relation to Christ, we must dig deep into our family roots from the perspective of truth, not just emotion. We must

> For us to truly experience a life worth living, we must take responsibility, not for what has been done to us, but for our reaction to what has been done to us.

choose to see those closest to us in the same way our heavenly Father does—as imperfect people who make imperfect choices. And we must take responsibility for our part in our own baggage and not just dump it all on someone else's doorstep.

For me, this means taking responsibility for the moments I lied to my parents, yelled at them, slammed the door in their faces, and completely disrespected them. I must take ownership for the moments I chose to believe the rank deceptions Satan breathed into my ear. I must take responsibility for my rebellion and disobedience when I knew good and well that what I was doing was wrong and that I was hurting myself and others.

For us to truly experience a life worth living, we must take responsibility, not for what has been done to us, but for our reaction to what has been done to us. As long as I focused on what had been done to me, I could never see clearly enough to discover what God wanted to do *within* me. It was not my fault that my parents chose to get divorced or that the high school senior chose to rape me. The fallen world we live in ensures that we will endure pain and hardship at the hands of others. It is a guarantee that people are going to hurt us in one way or another. If we do not learn how to respond rightly to those who hurt us, we will continue to live in misery and, because misery loves company, bring others right along with us.

> There is one sure antidote to self-pity over your past, and that is an awareness that, regardless of what has happened to you, you still belong to God.

The Bible offers a brilliant alternative to the world's way of dealing with suffering and unfair treatment:

> God is pleased with you when you do what you know is
> right and patiently endure unfair treatment. Of course,
> you get no credit for being patient if you are beaten for
> doing wrong. But if you suffer for doing good and endure it
> patiently, God is pleased with you. For God called you to do
> good, even if it means suffering, just as Christ suffered for
> you. He is your example, and you must follow in his steps.
>
> I PETER 2:19-21

As long as we focus on the wrongs done to us instead of bringing that hurt before the Lord, we will remain bitter and immobilized by the destructive force of self-pity. When we find ourselves sucked into this vortex of self-pity over things that have unjustly happened to us, our past is making us miserable in the present. And that, my friend, is on us! Psalm 73:21-22 describes that condition perfectly: "I realized that my heart was bitter, and I was all torn up inside. I was so foolish and ignorant—I must have seemed like a senseless animal to you." A self-pitying heart will inevitably grow bitter, and a bitter heart will inevitably grow cold, desensitizing us to the movement of God in our lives. In other words, a self-pitying heart can turn you stupid real quick.

There is one sure antidote to self-pity over your past, and that is an awareness that regardless of what has happened to you, you still belong to God. No matter what you witnessed in your childhood or what was done to you in your adolescence or what your family of origin was like, God remains near to you. This psalm puts it beautifully:

> Yet I still belong to you; you hold my right hand. You guide me with your counsel, leading me to a glorious destiny. Whom have I in heaven but you? I desire you more than anything on earth. My health may fail, and my spirit may grow weak, but God remains the strength of my heart; he is mine forever. PSALM 73:23-26

What amazes me about this passage is the realization that not only do *we* belong to *him* but that *he* belongs to *us*. The closing phrase of this verse sends a wave of awe through every pore on my body: "he is mine forever."

God is not simply a childhood fairy tale. He is the source of your breath and life. He is ever present, ever abiding, and ever capable. He chose you before the foundation of the earth was laid, and he knew the painful circumstances you would endure before the moon cast its first beam of light into the darkness.

We will see in future chapters how God can use every place of your hurt and pain to redeem it for his great purposes. But for now, may we rest in this truth:

YOU ARE NAMED BY GOD: *He is yours.*

CHAPTER 2

Pass It Down

THE MONTHS THAT FOLLOWED the birth of my daughter, Emma Grace, were some of the most emotional months of my life. For the most part, I was overwhelmed with the joy and delight of being on the receiving end of such a beautiful gift. But, if I am honest, I have to admit there were days when fear and doubt got the best of me. I remember sitting in my daughter's nursery and weeping over my small spiral notebook. As she slept, I penned a detailed list of all the harmful character traits I had witnessed in my life that I did not want my own child to see in me, her mom, as she grew up.

At the top of my list of generational patterns to sever was a lack of physical touch. As I was growing up, I didn't realize I had a problem expressing my love and affirmation through physical touch. In the home I was raised in, love and respect were shown through actions, such as washing the car or mowing the yard, but certainly not through warm embraces or sentimental touches.

It wasn't until I met the boyfriend who eventually became my husband that I realized how bankrupt my physical affection account was. Over the course of our dating relationship, he lovingly pointed out to me the ways it was ingrained in me to hold back from physical touch. This recognition shocked me and caused me to investigate my background. As it turns out, this lack of connection went back much further than my twenty years of living; it had been passed along for generations before me . . . by my mother, who struggled to show her love through physical affection, as well as my grandmother, who struggled with the same thing. (And from the stories I have heard, my great-grandmother was this way too.) It blows my mind how deeply these developmental patterns can run in a family's lineage.

> As we grow in maturity, we become no less infected by sin, but we do become more accountable for how we deal with the patterns we've been given.

As a mother myself, I want to make sure this generational infection stops with me. My desire is for my daughter, and now my son too, to catch a new legacy that they can pass on to their own children someday. Whether that means wrestling together on the living room rug or a long embrace before bed as I sing them a lullaby, I make the choice each day to heal, however gradually, this particular strand of infection in my family.

All of us, to one degree or another, have been on the receiving end of unhealthy behaviors and patterns. In your family it may be alcoholism, financial irresponsibility, infidelity, lying, negligence, or worry. Maybe it's scary territory for you to investigate generational sin. Perhaps even as you read this you feel trapped by a sense of inevitable doom that you'll repeat the same mistakes your parents or other family members made. If that's where you find yourself, take heart! You may feel cursed or corrupted, but in Christ, you are free.

Before we can look at our family members and the particular traits that have impacted who we are today, we must understand a bit about human nature in general. Here's the thing: no matter whom you were born to and how they impacted your life, the nature of the human family at large is corrupted. Just like a nasty stomach flu that comes home with your first grader and makes its way through all the members of your household, sin has been infecting humankind since the moment Adam and Eve came down with it in the first place and then passed it down to every generation since.

Therefore, the question is not whether our sinful lifestyle is the fault of the negative influences that surrounded us growing up, nor is the question whether we can avoid taking responsibility for our actions. The issue is how we will respond to the generational curses that have been passed on to us. As we grow in maturity and in our relationship with God, we become no less infected by sin, but we do become more accountable for how we deal with the patterns we've been given.

The biblical fact is that we carry the weight of sin from our very first breath. Romans 5:12-14 puts it this way:

When Adam sinned, sin entered the world. Adam's sin brought death, so death spread to everyone, for everyone sinned. Yes, people sinned even before the law was given. But it was not counted as sin because there was not yet any law to break. Still,

everyone died—from the time of Adam to the time of Moses—
even those who did not disobey an explicit commandment of
God, as Adam did. Now Adam is a symbol, a representation
of Christ, who was yet to come.

Paul describes Adam as a pattern, a cutout, of the one to come.
We are all born into the physical family of Adam, and although
you may have inherited your brown hair from your dad or your
blue eyes from your mom, Adam also left his mark on you: the
desire to sin. You may be saying to yourself, *This doesn't make any
sense. Why am I born into this world already condemned because of
someone else's disobedience?* Doesn't seem fair, does it? But like it or
not, we are made of the same stuff as Adam, and we are born into
a nature that is prone to rebel against God.

As I was growing up, Papa and Gran (my maternal grandparents) always said, "You don't have to teach a child to do wrong;
you only have to teach him to do right." Now that I am a mother
of two beautiful "heathens," I am able to see how true this statement is! At ten months old, my son had yet to take his first step
or speak any words beyond "Mama" or "Dada." He wore a diaper
24/7 because his neurotransmitters were not developed enough for
his brain to tell his body to go "tee-tee" and "poopy" in the potty.
But here is what he *did* know: he could scream so loud his face
would turn bright red when I did not put the food of his choice
in his mouth. He could make his body go completely stiff in anger
when I picked him up from a "no-no" area. And he could take any
toy away from his older sister whenever he desired to play with
it. Suffice it to say that our corrupted nature expresses itself from
birth. But that isn't the end of the story.

There is a great difference between Adam's sin and God's gracious gift. For the sin of this one man, Adam, brought death to many. But even greater is God's wonderful grace and his gift of forgiveness to many through this other man, Jesus Christ. . . . Yes, Adam's one sin brings condemnation for everyone, but Christ's one act of righteousness brings a right relationship with God and new life for everyone. Because one person disobeyed God, many became sinners. But because one other person obeyed God, many will be made righteous.

ROMANS 5:15, 18-19

There is another side to the inheritance of Adam, and that is the inheritance of Christ. Just as we were condemned by one act of sin, we are given life by one act of righteousness. Through condemning the human race through one man, God was able to save the human race through one man—Jesus Christ!

To the Third and Fourth Generation

In Exodus 3:14 the Lord presents himself to Moses as a self-existent, eternal being: "I AM WHO I AM." But in his next meeting with Moses, the Lord expresses not only his holiness but also his grace and goodness.

[The Lord] passed in front of Moses, proclaiming, "The LORD, the LORD, the compassionate and gracious God, slow to anger, abounding in love and faithfulness, maintaining love to thousands, and forgiving wickedness, rebellion and sin. Yet he does not leave the guilty unpunished; he punishes the children and their children for the sin of the parents to the third and fourth generation." EXODUS 34:6-7 (NIV)

Can you even begin to imagine the Lord of all majesty passing in front of you to give you a message? And as he passes by, having his voice resounding in your ears? When I imagine what the audible voice of the Lord would sound like in my presence, it gives me holy goose bumps!

The same God who knit you together is in complete control over where you've been, who you are, and who you will become.

If the Lord desired, he could have rained down fire from the sky, split the ground on which Moses was standing, or caused every mountain, river, and living creature to bow down in worship of his majesty and glory. But surprisingly, of all the characteristics God could have drawn attention to, he described himself as a "compassionate and gracious God, slow to anger, abounding in love and faithfulness." God chose to show his love above all the other attributes he possesses.

Many people think of God as a God of wrath—an old man with a long white beard who reclines in his Cracker Barrel rocker, throwing lightning bolts from heaven if we even *think* about doing something wrong. But God is quick to remind us that first and foremost he is a God who is loving, faithful, and forgiving.

However, if I am honest, there is something about that passage from Exodus that makes my brow lower just a bit and my nostrils flare (which they apparently tend to do when I feel frustrated or confused). I think to myself, *Why should my mother's sins, my father's sins, and for that matter, the sins of my grandparents and great-grandparents have any effect on who I am today?* And then an even more chilling thought comes to my mind, which causes my eyes to open wide: *And if their sins affect me, how will my sins affect my own beautiful children?*

To help us better understand God's plan and heart in this, let's read the following passage of Scripture:

> You shall not bow down to them or worship them; for I, the LORD your God, am a jealous God, punishing the children for the sin of the parents to the third and fourth generation of those who hate me, but showing love to a thousand generations of those who love me and keep my commandments. EXODUS 20:5-6 (NIV)

Just for a little background, it's important to understand that both passages give the same instruction, at two different times. Exodus 20:5-6 recounts God's first meeting to form a covenant (otherwise known as the Ten Commandments) between God and his chosen people, Israel. Exodus 34:6-7 describes Moses' second trip to the mountain after he found the Israelites partying around a golden calf.

The key to understanding both these Scripture passages is found in the words of Exodus 20:5: "of those who hate me" (NIV). The merciful Lord is telling us that it is not the repentant children who continue to receive the punishment; it is the children who follow in their parents' sinful footsteps. When children turn from the sinful ways of their parents and choose to obey God, they will not be punished for their parents' sins (see Ezekiel 18:14-20). But if the children continue to sin like their mothers and fathers, they will then share in the parents' punishment.

John Piper has a powerful way of bringing this concept home:

> When God visits the sins of the fathers on the children, he doesn't punish sinless children for the sins of their fathers.

He simply lets the effects of the fathers' sins take their natural course, infecting and corrupting the hearts of the children. For parents who love their children this is one of the most sobering texts in all the Bible. The more we let sin get the upper hand in our own lives, the more our children will suffer for it. Sin is like a contagious disease. My children don't suffer because I have it. They catch it from me and then suffer because they have it.[1]

Here's the deal—whether you blame God, your family, or yourself for the person you are right now, the fact remains that you have a disease. You are infected, and you cannot blame it away. And once you have the disease, you are a contagious carrier. Maybe your father was an angry, lying, depressed alcoholic, and your mother was bitter, divorced, and consumed with self-pity. If nothing blatant comes to mind immediately, don't underestimate the sins that often fly under the radar, like selfishness, materialism, and hypocrisy, which can be equally as destructive.

I pray, dear reader, that you are not feeling beaten down at this point, because we need to face up to the realities of sin before we can be set free from them. In the meantime, allow me to give you a little encouragement. God, the one who knit you together, the one who sent his Son into this world to shed his blood for you, the one who is in complete control of every moment under the sun—this same God is in complete control over where you've been, who you are, and who you will become.

As long as children are born into this sinful world and raised

---

1. John Piper, "The Lord, a God Merciful and Gracious" (sermon, October 7, 1984), http://www.desiringgod.org/resource-library/sermons/the-lord-a-god-merciful-and-gracious.

by sinners, there will always be the colossal need for a Savior. But thanks be to God, we *have* a Savior. Because of Christ's sacrifice on the cross, we have been given the power to break the chains of infection in our own lives and in the legacy we leave for those who come behind us. "He personally carried our sins in his body on the cross so that we can be dead to sin and live for what is right. By his wounds you are healed" (1 Peter 2:24).

You can't change the fact that you were born with this strain of infection any more than you can change the eye color you were born with. But you can choose to accept the true healing your heavenly Physician is offering you.

Take heart—he is the antibiotic for your infection!

YOU ARE NAMED BY GOD: *You are healed.*

CHAPTER 3

The Royal Family

GROWING UP, I WAS MORE OF A TOMBOY THAN A GIRLIE GIRL. I would rather have been outside playing "ninja" with my brother than in the house playing dress-up or dolls. I've never encouraged my daughter to wear pink or don a tiara, and yet somehow, with every fiber of her being, she believes she is a princess. She loves playing with dolls and dressing up, and just as naturally as breathing, she can color-coordinate her underwear to her outfit, which also matches her shoes and her hair bow. I love to peek through the crack in the door when she doesn't know I am there and watch her twirl around in her tulle dress-up gown—complete with matching shoes and crown, of course—as she sings aloud, "I am the princess of the castle, and I am beautiful . . . la la la la."

It's not just little girls who create alternate realities or sometimes even alternate identities. As adults, we do the same thing—although we've gotten a little better at being subtle about it. Every time we put on our everything-is-fine mask just to walk into the grocery store or to make it through the church service, we're trying to create a different reality for ourselves. Deep down we're hoping that if we imagine and play there long enough, maybe no one (including ourselves) will notice that we don't belong.

In 2 Samuel 13, you will find the story of King David; two of his sons, Amnon and Absalom; and their sister Tamar. David is king over Israel at this time. He has tons of wealth, heaps of success, and the love and respect of the people who follow him.

Can you imagine being one of his royal children? Sounds like a piece of cake, right? *No worries*, you'd think. You'd have your every need attended to, and you'd be looked on as the rock star of your town. Surely, growing up in an environment like that, a royal child wouldn't have enough daily stress to lead to sin.

Oh, but wait a minute! Although these folks are royal, and although they are in the Bible, they are still *infected*. The simple truth is that there are consequences to this sin infection that plagues us, whether we're royalty or commoners. As we talk about this royal family's story, let's focus on a few points we can apply to our own lives:

- There is no such thing as a secret sin. Like an infection, sin starts small, in the private places of our thoughts. But like any kind of infection, it soon spreads inside us and contaminates those around us.
- Sin affects everyone—even those we never intended to hurt. We must break the cycles of sin in our lives and allow God to break *us* so our poor choices don't affect those who come after us, such as our children and grandchildren.

- There are always consequences for our sin. Although it may sometimes feel as if God is harshly punishing us for our sin, the Bible tells us to look at those consequences as discipline (see Hebrews 12:7-8). God disciplines us the way parents correct and instruct their children when they go astray.

In 2 Samuel we see what happens when a highly contagious father spreads his infection to his children and when children, in turn, refuse to seek treatment. Let's take a peek together.

> In the course of time, Amnon son of David fell in love with Tamar, the beautiful sister of Absalom son of David.
>
> 2 SAMUEL 13:1 (NIV)

Note that verse 1 tells us that Amnon falls in love with Tamar, his half sister, "in the course of time." Allow me to fill you in on a little-known fact about time: it can be a breeding ground for sin. If we aren't vigilant about how we're spending our hours and days, the idle passing of time can be an effective weapon in Satan's armory. Unless we are focused completely on what the Lord desires of us, we'll soon be twiddling our thumbs of spiritual complacency—which is exactly where Satan starts spinning webs of fatal desire. Plainly put, Satan desires all-consuming sin to creep into our lives, ultimately resulting in death. Of course, a believer's *physical* death would give the enemy a reason to boast. However, what delights Satan and his minions all the more is when he succeeds in making us what I call the "walking dead"—in other words, Christians who have sat their stagnant rear ends on the sidelines in the middle of the most important game of the season.

So Amnon has time on his hands. He might have helped his dad out with a few battles here and there, but for the most part, he is a prince with too much time and too little to do. His half sister, Tamar, is beautiful to look at, and Amnon spends his time doing just that. He allows himself to become obsessed with sexual desire for her.

> Amnon became so obsessed with Tamar that he became ill.
> She was a virgin, and Amnon thought he could never have her.
> But Amnon had a very crafty friend—his cousin Jonadab. He
> was the son of David's brother Shimea. One day Jonadab said
> to Amnon, "What's the trouble? Why should the son of a king
> look so dejected morning after morning?" So Amnon told him,
> "I am in love with Tamar, my brother Absalom's sister."
>
> 2 SAMUEL 13:2-4

Ha! Amnon thinks he's in love with Tamar? Give me a break. The dude's making himself physically sick from thinking about the girl and is walking around the palace looking all haggard and pitiful. Sounds like love to me (big wink)! Prince Amnon has an unfortunate case of lust, not love. Lust requires immediate satisfaction; love, as 1 Corinthians 13 puts it, is patient.

We also notice in this passage that Amnon confides in his "crafty" cousin Jonadab. No doubt Amnon knows Jonadab's reputation, and he likely asked for his advice in the past. Is it possible he is looking for someone to back up what his itching ears want to hear?

And so we need to examine our own counselors too. Where do we turn for advice or direction? Are we truly seeking godly wisdom, or are we looking for someone to affirm our sinful tendencies? Like Amnon, many of us tend to run straight to a family member or close friend for guidance when the storms of life begin to rumble. Please do not misunderstand—when you're having a bad day or struggling with a serious issue, there is nothing quite like the loving consolation of a mother; the piercing, Spirit-filled words of a father; or the shared tears of a reliable sibling or trusted friend. And although it is wise to seek counsel from trusted family members during difficult times, those people shouldn't be the first ones we run to. The Lord himself should be our number-one source for wisdom. And when we do get guidance from friends and family members, we must run every piece of input through the filter of God's Word.

In his obsession, Amnon heeds the words of his cousin Jonadab, who basically tells Amnon (I'm paraphrasing here), "Pretend to be sick [as if he had much pretending to do]. Lie down in your royal bed, and when your dad comes to check on you, tell him you want Tamar to make you something to eat and bring it to you herself." Amnon does just that (verse 6).

As directed by the king, Tamar brings the food and prepares it before Amnon. I can't help but wonder about all the servants standing around the palace.

> When Tamar arrived at Amnon's house, she went to the place where he was lying down so he could watch her mix some dough. Then she baked his favorite dish for him. But when she set the serving tray before him, he refused to eat.
>
> 2 SAMUEL 13:8-9

What? Tamar comes all this way, brings her pan and dough, goes to all the trouble to make the bread in front of Amnon, and then he refuses to eat it? Of course he does. Remember, it has never been about the food in the first place.

Verse 9 says that upon Tamar's arrival, Amnon tells everyone to get out. They all must have thought it strange that Amnon wants to be left alone with his beautiful sister—in his bedroom, of all places. A small twinge of curiosity, possibly guilt, no doubt passes through the pits of their stomachs as they follow orders and close the door. And here we are—at the scene of the crime. Don't you just want to call a time-out on Tamar's behalf? Wouldn't you love to run in and yell, "Watch out, Tamar—something bad is about to happen to you"?

When I get to this part of the story, I am reminded of those television commercials that portray two window-replacement guys wearing thick gloves and carrying a huge sheet of glass. They are carefully carrying this perfectly cut piece of glass to some unknown destination. As they walk cautiously, grasping the sharp edges, it seems there is always unwanted chaos swirling around them—people bustling through the streets, a dog chasing a cat, children playing catch, a ball soaring through the air. You know something's coming, right? You can see the fate of the glass unfolding before you, and you would love to jump out of your seat and yell, "Watch out, guys!" The thing about glass is that once it's shattered, it is impossible to piece it back together.

> God's standards for morality are not suspended just because we are dealing with family.

Back to our story:

Amnon is so consumed with sinful desire for his sister that he grabs the hand she reaches out to serve him with and blurts, "Come to bed with me, my darling sister" (2 Samuel 13:11).

After the rape, Amnon realizes he doesn't *love* his sister but actually *hates* her. He sends her away with a shout, "Get out of here!" (verse 15), paying no attention to the fact that he has now singlehandedly ruined the rest of her life. What a day for poor Tamar. She begins her morning thinking she is simply going to help her sick brother, and by the end of the day finds herself humiliated and ruined. Tamar has been defiled by a sin strictly forbidden by God, making her chances of being married in that culture slim to none.

Enter big brother Absalom. Absalom is the third son of King David and the full brother of Tamar. As we learn in 2 Samuel, he is protective not only of his sister's integrity but of his father's kingdom as well. Surely this guy's got some good advice, right?

> Her brother Absalom saw her and asked, "Is it true that Amnon has been with you? Well, my sister, keep quiet for now, since he's your brother. Don't you worry about it." So Tamar lived as a desolate woman in her brother Absalom's house.
>
> 2 SAMUEL 13:20

Absalom pretty much tells Tamar, "Don't worry about it; it's a family thing." Although Absalom is trying to comfort his sister, he downplays the situation—and the sin—by treating it as a family matter, not a *God* matter.

Have you ever had a family member give you good comfort but bad advice? Often our family members are more concerned about protecting a reputation or the family name than about facing sin for what it is—*sin*. God's standards for morality are not suspended just because we are dealing with family.

As this story progresses and we hear from various sides—brother, sister, cousin—you might be wondering, *Where's good ol' Dad in all of this? You know, King David, the ruler over the entire nation of Israel?*

> When King David heard what had happened, he was very angry. And though Absalom never spoke to Amnon about this, he hated Amnon deeply because of what he had done to his sister. 2 SAMUEL 13:21-22

Finally! Dad hears what has happened. (Don't parents always find out?) This is the moment we've been waiting for, right? Surely King David will put a royal stop to all this household drama. I mean, he is the king, after all. He commands armies, runs the government, conquers nations—he should be able to get a tight rein on his son Amnon, who seems to be running around in the mud and getting filthy with sin.

But wait. Poor David, Lord love him (and he does, very much), has a disease. Yes, David was the greatest king of Israel and an ancestor of Jesus Christ. He is listed in the spiritual hall of fame (see Hebrews 11) and is described as a man after God's own heart (see 1 Samuel 13:14). But he is also infected with sin, and his symptoms include lust, adultery, murder, disobedience, and ineffective discipline of his children.

The Bible is surprisingly silent about what happens to David's family in the next couple of years. Much to my dismay, the story suddenly jumps to the next scene, with the "two years later" blurb at the bottom of the screen.

> Two years later, when Absalom's sheep were being sheared at
> Baal-hazor near Ephraim, Absalom invited all the king's sons to
> come to a feast. 2 SAMUEL 13:23

Two years pass after this horrible incident takes place. And in all that time, David does nothing to rectify what has happened in his family. One might be inclined to say, "Well, maybe David didn't hear the complete story. Maybe he didn't realize how bad the situation really was." But the Bible gives no indication of this. In fact, Scripture states the contrary: "When King David heard what had happened . . ." (verse 21). David is fully aware of what happened between his royal children, and although he is not happy about it, he stands by and makes one of the biggest parenting mistakes in the books.

He does nothing.

So what could have possibly happened over the course of David's life that would lead him to be so complacent when dealing with his rebellious children? Stay with me in this, friends, as we journey back through David's history.

The Legacy of King David

All seven of Jesse's sons were presented to Samuel. But Samuel said to Jesse, "The LORD has not chosen any of these." Then Samuel asked, "Are these all the sons you have?"

"There is still the youngest," Jesse replied. "But he's out in the fields watching the sheep and goats."

"Send for him at once," Samuel said. "We will not sit down to eat until he arrives."

So Jesse sent for him. He was dark and handsome, with beautiful eyes.

And the LORD said, "This is the one; anoint him."

So as David stood there among his brothers, Samuel took the flask of olive oil he had brought and anointed David with the oil. And the Spirit of the LORD came powerfully upon David from that day on. Then Samuel returned to Ramah.

1 SAMUEL 16:10-13

As we rewind the tape to the beginning of David's life, let's see if we can find parallels between his story and what happens to his children. Note the special blessings and also the generational curses that plague this royal family.

David enters the scene as a young boy, "dark and handsome, with beautiful eyes." David is fresh out of the field, where he tends sheep, when he is handpicked by God. He may be young, but he is talented—not only at fending off wild animals but also at playing beautiful music on the harp for Saul, the current king (see 1 Samuel 16:18). And it isn't long before his talents go public.

As Goliath moved closer to attack, David quickly ran out to meet him. Reaching into his shepherd's bag and taking out a stone, he hurled it with his sling and hit the Philistine in the forehead. The stone sank in, and Goliath stumbled and fell face down on the ground. So David triumphed over the Philistine with only a sling and a stone, for he had no sword.

1 SAMUEL 17:48-50

Many of us know this story from our childhood. I remember hearing it when I was an earnest seven-year-old attending vacation Bible school. I would work intently at craft time to glue little felt stones to the tiny felt David so that he could *gently* lob the stones at

the felt Goliath (not to hurt him, of course—just to scare him away).
It wasn't until I was much older and read 1 Samuel 17 for myself
that I realized my dear Bible teachers were desperately attempting
to downplay an R-rated story into a G-rated version.

David doesn't just kill Goliath—he kills him *dead*. Beginning in
chapter 18, we see that King Saul gains a new appreciation for the
young David. David single-handedly kills the giant Philistine who
led his people as they gathered their forces against Saul's armies.
Verse 2 tells us, "From that day on
Saul kept David with him." Well, now,
wouldn't you?

First Samuel continues to tell the
winding saga of David and Saul. Saul
may be a strong, rich, and powerful
king, but he is decaying on the inside,
and it isn't long before his physical death follows. In the shadow
of Saul's death, David becomes king of the entire nation of Israel.
And throughout David's rise to royalty, the Lord stays with him,
protecting him and blessing him.

> It should give us great hope to know that even God's anointed men and women had their moments of weakness, failings, and sins.

Something we often fail to see is that God's blessings are rarely
confined to just our own lifetime. As we see in the legacy of David,
God chooses David to be the line through whom the Savior would
be born—impacting all generations to come until the end of the age.

> You will conceive and give birth to a son, and you are to call
> him Jesus. He will be great and will be called the Son of the
> Most High. The Lord God will give him the throne of his
> father David, and he will reign over Jacob's descendants forever;
> his kingdom will never end. LUKE 1:31-33 (NIV)

When God promises David that his kingdom will last forever, he isn't kidding. No earthly kingdom could last forever, but the Kingdom being referred to in this passage is a *supernatural* one. It is the eternal, indescribable place in which Christ will reign.

Wow! Can you imagine being handpicked for a task like this by the Lord God himself? David's life and reign are clearly marked by the Lord's blessing. He goes on to conquer many nations and win countless wars, achieving victory after victory. To put it in layman's terms, David is quite the superstar.

However, as time goes on—and remember what I said earlier about time—David gets so busy working toward the prosperity of his nation and strengthening the nation with military power that it makes a person wonder if he has any time left to strengthen his own relationship with the Lord.

In the spring of the year, when kings normally go out to war, David sent Joab and the Israelite army to fight the Ammonites. They destroyed the Ammonite army and laid siege to the city of Rabbah. However, David stayed behind in Jerusalem.

Late one afternoon, after his midday rest, David got out of bed and was walking on the roof of the palace. As he looked out over the city, he noticed a woman of unusual beauty taking a bath. He sent someone to find out who she was, and he was told, "She is Bathsheba, the daughter of Eliam and the wife of Uriah the Hittite." Then David sent messengers to get her; and when she came to the palace, he slept with her. She had just completed the purification rites after having her menstrual period. Then she returned home. Later, when Bathsheba discovered that she was pregnant, she sent David a message, saying, "I'm pregnant." 2 SAMUEL 11:1-5

Take a look at that first verse again. Is David not a king? Is it not his time to go off to war? It's hard to say for sure, but it looks like David's power and success are getting to his head a little. Instead of leading his troops into battle, David opts to take some time off, get a little R & R. And you know what happens when you go on vacation. Your sleep schedule gets all out of whack. So one afternoon, after taking a nap, David takes a stroll on the roof of the palace. He sees a woman bathing, and instead of "bouncing his eyes," as my husband would say, he takes another look, then another, and then just plain gawks at her beauty.

When David finds out she's married, that should have ended it for him then and there. But here's where that sinful nature takes over and the infection begins to spread. Perhaps David was once in a consistent routine of taking his spiritual medicine. But things got busy. You know—battles to win, governments to run, nations to lead. And ever so subtly, the infection began to spread into his mind, severely crippling his thoughts. And from his thoughts, it progressed to his actions.

And what of Bathsheba's husband, also one of David's servants? Loyal Uriah is busy fighting on the front lines of a battle that David, his commander in chief, didn't bother to show up to!

As a result of his own track record of sinful choices, David fails to teach his children the ways of the Lord. His sins and the guilt he carries from them hinder him from rightly disciplining his sons and daughters when their sins begin to mirror his own. Take special note here—the very temptations David dealt with in his younger years are the same ones he has passed down to his children. The unfortunate truth is that David's sins prove to be his family's undoing.

- David: lust and adultery with Bathsheba à Amnon: lust and rape of Tamar
- David: murder of Bathsheba's husband, Uriah à Absalom: murder of his brother Amnon (see 2 Samuel 13:23-29)
- David: ineffective guidance and direction of his children à Absalom: ineffective guidance of Tamar
- David: disobedience to God à David's family: disobedience to God

As we read the life story of David, we meet a man who has committed adultery, had a man murdered to cover up his sin, and started a chain of generational sin. David also suffers painful consequences for his sin for the rest of his life—and so do his children.

However, when David seeks the face of the Lord in authentic sorrow and repentance, the Lord creates for David a new beginning as he lavishes his grace upon him.

It is no surprise that David later writes these words:

He forgives all my sins and heals all my diseases.
He redeems me from death and crowns me with love and tender mercies.
He fills my life with good things. My youth is renewed like the eagle's! PSALM 103:3-5

The Bible always tells the beautiful and brutal truth about people and the human condition. It should give us great hope to know that even God's anointed men and women had their moments of weakness, failings, and sins. If he could use them, it follows that he can use the likes of us, too—shortcomings and all.

Through the work of Jesus Christ, God is able to save lost sinners, forgive disobedient saints, and even go a step further to redeem the pitfalls from our past.

As we close the final chapters of David's life, it is not his sinful shortcomings that receive the spotlight; it is the deliverance and reward he receives from the Lord.

> The LORD lives! Praise to my Rock! May God, the Rock of my salvation, be exalted! He is the God who pays back those who harm me; he brings down the nations under me and delivers me from my enemies. You hold me safe beyond the reach of my enemies; you save me from violent opponents. For this, O LORD, I will praise you among the nations; I will sing praises to your name. You give great victories to your king; you show unfailing love to your anointed, to David and all his descendants forever. 2 SAMUEL 22:47-51

Despite David's past, the Lord enables him to leave a legacy of leadership, spiritual passion, kingship, and an eternal Kingdom. Even with all his flaws, David has gone down in history as a man after God's own heart.

The same can be true for you, too. God can give you a new legacy and allow you to pass on a blessing, not a curse, to the next generation.

> YOU ARE NAMED BY GOD:
> *You are more than the sum of your mistakes.*

CHAPTER 4

Collision Course

MY BODY WAS FROZEN, yet I could feel the subtle tingle that seemed to be making its way to the surface of my skin. Why was I shaking? I wasn't cold. My bare legs were folded tightly against my bare chest, my chin resting on my knees. My eyes were fixed on the steady stream of water pouring from the faucet. The steady sound of water trickling into the tub somehow comforted me, as if I were far away, near a tranquil, flowing stream.

My brain told me that the water was verging on scalding, but I was shaking uncontrollably, like I was in the middle of a snowstorm. How long had I been sitting here? I didn't even remember undressing and turning the faucet handle. I blinked for the first time in what seemed like hours. My brow crinkled as my gaze turned from the clear stream flowing into the tub to the tinted water pooling around my body. In astonishment and confusion,

I dipped my hands into the bath and watched as the water collected in my palm. Red—the water was red. I rose quickly to my feet. What was happening? Why was the water colored with blood? And why were my wrists and neck so tender to the touch?

Suddenly my near-comatose state was shattered. Every painful memory and sensation rushed over me. I dropped the weight of my body back into the bath, sending a wave of water over the side onto the cold tile floor. I felt like a spectator of my own life, wanting desperately to leave but chained to my seat and forced to watch.

I replayed the scene over and over in my mind. It had all happened so fast. I had trusted him to take care of me. I had believed he would keep me safe. I had told him no. I told him no again. And I told him, with even more intensity, no again.

In that brief moment, I was forever changed. The damage had been done without my consent, but I could not undo it. I was young, but I had seen the red flags telling me to get away. Yet I was so desperate to be loved by another human being that I ignored all the warning signs. And that's how I found myself in that place, with that man, who took from me a gift that could never be returned.

. . .

Whether we like it or not, our past experiences affect who we are in the here and now. Whether those are experiences we've intentionally sought out or things that have happened to us without our permission, they make an impact on the way we view life—and ourselves. And in almost every case, the most painful things we undergo involve other people, whether they've hurt us or we've hurt them. In a way, humans are like cars stuck in high gear—at some point we're going to crash into one another. We dent each other's fenders, smash each other's headlights, and cause great damage when we collide into each other.

The traumatic experience of being raped at the age of fifteen set me on a course bound for many more head-on collisions. In that one moment, a seed was planted in me that changed my perception of myself and what I was worth.

For the first few months afterward I was in such a state of shock and confusion that I allowed the relationship with this boy to continue—partly because I thought we now had to get married, and partly because I was terrified that no other man would desire "damaged goods." Each encounter with him was an emotionless blur. Whenever I cast my gaze to the floor and mumbled, "Please, not again. Not this time," there was no respect, no release. Each time I felt tainted and abused all over again. And utterly helpless.

No matter how far we've drifted, it's never too far for our loving and compassionate God to pursue us and find us.

I was screaming inside to tell someone how I was feeling—to ask if this "relationship" was normal. Having never even kissed a boy prior to this, and having never had "the talk" with my parents, I simply could not comprehend where to go from this point. I was convinced that no one would believe me if I told them I had been raped by this young man. And so I didn't tell . . . not a soul.

We eventually broke up. He moved on, and I pretended to move on by dating other guys and trying to shove memories of that night deep inside. But when I looked in the mirror, I detested myself for who I had become, for allowing myself to be treated like a victim.

During the high school years that followed, those roots of bitterness and self-doubt took hold of me, suffocating the truth of Christ within me and growing into a thorny garden of bad decisions and heartache. It was four years before I spoke a word to anyone about that night. And for those four years, that night became the focus of my existence and my identity. I was trapped in my bondage, desperate to escape but never embracing the freedom my God was offering me.

Finally, though, my eyes were opened to the truth that, no matter how far we've drifted, it's never too far for our loving and compassionate God to pursue us and find us. The Lord's pressing on my spirit inevitably brought me to the point where I was forced to make a choice: take God up on his offer of freedom and get on with living, or remain trapped by the chains of doubt and fear and miss out on everything he had in store for me. By the grace of God, I did experience healing and freedom, but only once I was willing to look back and deal with my past.

There is a significant difference between people who *reflect* on their past and those who *ruminate* on it. Reflection can be healthy when we are able to look back without being thrown off track for the future. Ruminating, however, can be lethal, for as long as we remain obsessed with who we once were, we will never make the choice to change into who God desires us to be.

In the aftermath of emotional or physical trauma, we tend to forget a crucial point about the past—*it is the past*. Our past is much like a piece of wood, with lines and grains deeply embedded in it. Those grooves are a unique part of what gives us our character and sets us apart from every other person who has walked this earth. No matter how diligently we might sand away at that piece of wood, those markings remain ingrained deep in the core of our being. We can't go back and change those circumstances in our past that have marked us, but God can take those scars and polish them until they are transformed into something beautiful.

Dealing with the Wreckage

In this chapter we will focus on overcoming the painful parts of our past—whether they're a result of rotten circumstances or wrongs done against us. To some degree or another, all of us have been hurt by other human beings. We have all been caught in collisions with people that resulted in either immediate or future disaster for us. Some of us saw the warning signs: "Beware—dangerous curve ahead!" But others of us were caught completely off guard by the headlights that were suddenly bearing down on us from the oncoming lane.

As I write these words, my eyes are filled with tears. I think about the many scenarios in which innocent victims suffer as a result of others' vicious attacks. Nothing is quite as painful as when someone else's sin seeps over and impacts us or those close to us. The aftermath of these experiences can leave us feeling wounded, shocked, fearful, and confused. Our minds swim with questions like "How could he do that to me?" "How can I ever trust that person again?" "How can I go on after this?"

> We can't go back and change the circumstances in our past that have marked us, but God can take those scars and polish them until they are transformed into something beautiful.

By the grace of God, maybe you have already cleaned up much of the wreckage from your past and are back on track again. If that's the case, praise God for the forgiveness you have been able to bestow and the love he has equipped you with in order to move forward. Or maybe you still find yourself stuck at the scene of the crash, with broken glass and dented metal littering your path. Either way, I believe God has something to teach all of us on our journey toward redeeming the painful events of our past.

God is no stranger to human suffering. Scripture is filled with accounts of innocent victims who were caught off guard by the sin-filled attacks of others. But of all the names that grace the pages of the Bible, one in particular stands out to me as an example of someone who endured intense suffering. If there was ever someone who was caught in a literal onslaught of destruction and devastation, this would be the man. In fact, his anguish was so intense that it fills an entire book of the Bible. Yep, forty-two whole chapters are devoted to this man's encounter with suffering—and eventually to God's goodness shining through the wreckage.

What strikes me most about this biblical account is not just the extent of this man's suffering but the origin of it. When we experience pain as the result of another human being's sin, it can be quite devastating. Even more damaging, perhaps, is a blow of suffering that comes directly from the hand of Satan. And now let me rock your world just a bit more. What would you say about someone who experiences suffering not only because of someone else's sin or because of Satan's attacks but ultimately because God the Father *allows* the hardship to take place?

Yes, you read that right.

Our loving and merciful God is standing by, totally sovereign and in control of the situation, but allowing the devastation to take place. Now before you get your feathers ruffled, I want to assure you I'm not blaming God for the suffering in the world. Hang with me for a few more pages. This is good stuff!

Lessons From the Life of Job

One day the members of the heavenly court came to present themselves before the LORD, and the Accuser, Satan, came with them. "Where have you come from?" the LORD asked Satan.

Satan answered the LORD, "I have been patrolling the earth, watching everything that's going on."

Then the LORD asked Satan, "Have you noticed my servant Job? He is the finest man in all the earth. He is blameless— a man of complete integrity. He fears God and stays away from evil." JOB 1:6-8

There are two major points I'd like us to take away from this. The first is that Job is a godly man, unlike anyone else on earth. God goes so far as to say that Job is "blameless." (How many of us can say we have that kind of track record before God?) The story of Job is proof that bad things do happen to good people.

One day when Job's sons and daughters were feasting at the oldest brother's house, a messenger arrived at Job's home with this news: "Your oxen were plowing, with the donkeys feeding beside them, when the Sabeans raided us. They stole all the animals and killed all the farmhands. I am the only one who escaped to tell you."

While he was still speaking, another messenger arrived with this news: "The fire of God has fallen from heaven and burned up your sheep and all the shepherds. I am the only one who escaped to tell you."

While he was still speaking, a third messenger arrived with this news: "Three bands of Chaldean raiders have stolen your camels and killed your servants. I am the only one who escaped to tell you."

While he was still speaking, another messenger arrived with this news: "Your sons and daughters were feasting in their oldest brother's home. Suddenly, a powerful wind swept in from the wilderness and hit the house on all sides. The house collapsed, and all your children are dead. I am the only one who escaped to tell you." JOB 1:13-19

If you're anything like me, you have to pause for a deep breath at this point. Doesn't this read like a science-fiction novel? And let's put it into perspective even more. The average person doesn't experience the extent of suffering in an entire lifetime that Job endures over this short time period. Much of the loss Job experiences all happens in one day!

The second point I'd like us to take away deals with the outstanding character of Job. The text says, "In all of this, Job did not sin by blaming God" (Job 1:22). Attempt to put yourself in Job's shoes for a moment (although none of us would ever want to be there). In a short period of time, Job's entire life comes crashing down around him. His animals, which in his day are a man's livelihood, are completely wiped out. Job's employees (or servants), some of whom are no doubt his friends, are either murdered or burned. All of Job's children are killed in a horrible storm. And as if that isn't enough, in the next chapter we find out that Job is infected with itching, festering sores all over his skin. The sores are so excruciating that Job breaks off a piece of pottery in order to scrape away the painful flesh that torments him night and day (see Job 2:7-8).

Perhaps the most striking thing about Job's story is not the tragedies he faces, however. What stands out to me is his initial response to suffering: "The LORD gave me what I had, and the LORD has taken it away. Praise the name of the LORD!" (Job 1:21).

Be honest with yourself here. You alone know the suffering you have personally endured. No other person in this world can tell you that a particular circumstance in your life was not, or should not have been, a tragedy. If it was suffering to you, then it was suffering. As you think back on those difficult moments in your life, whether self-inflicted or others induced, in which circumstances did you praise God at the crash site? In that moment—not in the days or weeks or years after, but in *that* moment—did you lift your eyes to the heavens? Did you call out the beautiful name of Jesus? Did your knees hit the ground in reverence to the all-knowing one? Like Job, were you able to acknowledge the sovereign authority the Lord has over everything he gave to us in the first place? Like Job, were you able to praise God not only for being the one who blesses us with an abundance of wealth, health, and happiness, but also for being the one who can take away those blessings as he sees fit?

Since we're being honest with one another here, I can think of very few times in my life in which I have praised God right there

> Your Creator knows your suffering before you ever endure it.

in the midst of the storm. I wonder how differently my personal storms would have impacted my future if I had taken my pain to God immediately, right there in the middle of the sirens and shattered pieces of glass.

It's true that the book of the Bible bears Job's name, but as I look at the drama unfolding on the pages, it is not Job who should walk away with the leading role.

The role of VICTIM: Played by Job, a man who is living life right. He is so good, in fact, that there is not another man on the earth who lives up to his standards.

The role of VILLAIN: Played by Satan, who is up to no good, roaming the earth and looking for the next person to deceive. Poor Satan (sarcasm intended)! Although he would like to believe he is in control, he is subject to the Lord's will.

The role of BOSS MAN: Played by God. Note that it is not Satan but God who first mentions Job (1:8). At first read, you might question why a loving God would allow a blameless person such as Job to endure such tribulation. That's a valid question, which we will unpack soon.

Your Creator knows your suffering before you ever endure it. He alone allows it, and he is fully aware of Satan's attempts to bring difficulty upon you. As you face hardships and struggles, you must never doubt God's compassion. As we press on through our hurt, he bears our grief right along with us. And he has a grander purpose for those trials—to draw us deeper with him.

Most encouraging of all, Jesus is no stranger to suffering himself. Isaiah gives us this picture of the Messiah:

> He was despised and rejected—a man of sorrows, acquainted with deepest grief. We turned our backs on him and looked the other way. He was despised, and we did not care. Yet it was our weaknesses he carried; it was our sorrows that weighed him down. And we thought his troubles were a punishment from God, a punishment for his own sins! But he was pierced for our rebellion, crushed for our sins. He was beaten so we could be whole. He was whipped so we could be healed. ISAIAH 53:3-5

Jesus alone holds the title of ultimate suffering endured.

YOU ARE NAMED BY GOD: *You are not alone.*

CHAPTER 5

Where Is God in Your Pain?

THREE YEARS AGO MY PRECIOUS MOTHER was diagnosed with an aggressive form of cancer at the age of fifty. Instead of soaking my pillow with pools of tears, I found myself taking on the role of a crime-scene investigator. My mother was diagnosed with one of the rarest forms of cancer—multiple myeloma. To make matters all the more alarming, when the doctors finally found the cancer, it had already progressed to stage four.

In my research, I learned that multiple myeloma is an infestation of the plasma cells, and it is most common among African American males over the age of sixty. The doctors informed us that myeloma is treatable but incurable.

I will never forget the moment I walked into my mother's bedroom, holding back my tears, charged with the daunting task of telling my mother personally not only that she had cancer but that it had already reached stage four. She had been scheduled to have an appointment with our local oncologist to find out whether the tests showed she had cancer cells. On the day of her appointment, however, she was too weak to walk, much less ride in a car to the doctor's office. We didn't know it at that point, but that was because her bones literally had holes in them. My grandparents and I took on the task of meeting with the doctor to find out the results, and it fell to me to break the news to her.

God is not intimidated by our questions, but it's up to us to ask them.

You think I had questions?

Oh yeah, I had some questions! My mother was an otherwise healthy fifty-year-old Caucasian female who took her vitamin supplements and had no history of osteoporosis—far from the typical profile of this disease. Let me tell you, I was so consumed with questions for God that I had absolutely no time to cry about the situation. I was pregnant at the time, and so was my sister-in-law. I desperately wanted my mom, otherwise known as Nana, to have several more decades to love on and pray for her grandchildren. Why this? Why now?

It was truly an unavoidable disaster placed in our lives without any warning. It was a Job moment of my own, and I had to decide how I would respond. Would I acknowledge God as sovereign and praise him, or would I turn my back on him in bitterness?

Please allow me to be transparent for a moment. I believe Scripture is clear that there are times to be sad, angry, quiet, and grieved over your circumstances (see Ecclesiastes 3:4), and I experienced all of those emotions during the first few days of emergency room visits with my mother. So when I talk about praising the Lord,

I don't mean being in denial or responding to my mother's cancer with laughter and dancing. In this case, praising God for me meant choosing to see him in the circumstance—staying faithful to him in the midst of uncertainty. I may not have been praising him with joyful music or celebration, but I praised him through my tears and my grief. I praised him by staying close to him when I could have run.

At one point after Mom was diagnosed, I was able to praise God that her bones started breaking. You see, she had been feeling fine up to that point, and this was the only indicator that sent the doctors in search of this particular cancer in her cells. Had her bones not inexplicably broken, they might not have found her cancer in time to treat it. Thankfully my mom was able to get a bone marrow transplant, which allowed her a few more months on this earth to celebrate the arrival of two of her grandchildren.

As we discussed in the last chapter, bad things happen to good people. Job is proof positive of that. We have also established that our heavenly Father is not necessarily the responsible party behind the disaster brought our way, but he *is* completely in control of any and every situation. He allows suffering to exist in our lives. But as humans, we are born with an insatiable need for answers. We are desperate to know *why*. Is there a purpose for our suffering? And what do we do when there seems to be no cause for the wreckage in our lives? Job puts his question to God this way: "If I have sinned, what have I done to you, O watcher of all humanity? Why make me your target? Am I a burden to you?" (Job 7:20).

Perhaps you have found yourself in a similar place of questioning God in the midst of suffering. I assure you that when an attack takes place in your life, it is common to be left with shreds of confusion. God is not intimidated by our questions, but it's up to us to ask them. We can't just bury our grievances against God and expect that they'll disappear somehow. In order for us to adequately deal with the moments of victimization or tragedy from our past, we must take time to search our own hearts and minds now, in the present.

Have you put your pain to rest with the Lord, or do you still have some unresolved questions for him? When you're in the midst of suffering, you may wonder:

Is God mad at me?
Has God abandoned me?
What did I do to deserve this?

And perhaps the most common question of all in the middle of suffering is the one Job asks—that simple but loaded *Why?* The truth is that suffering may have a number of different causes—our own sin, the sin of others, circumstances, the hand of God, or an attack by Satan. But as we've learned from Job, the big question shouldn't be *Why?* The more important question really is *Who?* Suffering has a higher purpose in your life, and that's to cause you to trust God for who he is, not what he can do.

As a woman, I ask a lot of questions—not just in times of suffering, but in the small things as well (my desire for all the details can drive my husband crazy!). And when a pain-evoking event takes place in my life or in the lives of the ones I hold dear, I seem to have a notebook full of questions for God. As a woman, I also desire security. I feel sure that the more details I know regarding a particular situation, the more secure I will feel about it. For me, being informed equals being secure.

With the news of my mother's cancer, God answered me the same way he answers Paul in 2 Corinthians 12:9 when Paul is begging the Lord to take away his "thorn in his flesh." We are unsure exactly what this thorn is that Paul is struggling with—perhaps a chronic pain, opposition he has met along the way, a certain temptation, or another kind of trouble. The specifics don't really matter—you may replace this with whatever your thorn may be at the moment. As grievous as the suffering is for Paul, the sovereign Lord lets it continue. God knows of the good that would one day come out of this evil, and he answers Paul in the same way he answers us: "My grace is sufficient for you, for my power is made perfect in weakness" (NIV).

God does not take away Paul's pain but instead assures Paul that he will equip him with enough grace and strength to endure his suffering. Not only that, but if Paul continues to rely on him, God will bring Paul face-to-face with his perfect power. God didn't answer my prayer to **It is better to know God** heal my mother, and he never told me **than to know the answers!** why I had to lose my mother to cancer at such a young age. But he did tell me that he was enough. I grasped the *who*, and that was enough when I didn't understand the *why*.

What I have learned along the way, and what Job learned too, is that it is better to know God than to know the answers!

As we read chapters 38–41 of Job, we catch a true glimpse of God's goodness and ultimate control as he personally responds to Job's questions. When Job asks God why he has to endure such extreme suffering, God doesn't answer with a point-by-point explanation about each of Job's losses. Instead, he asks Job his own series of questions, and in doing so, he turns the focus from

Job to God himself. God doesn't minimize Job's pain, but he does give him a bigger picture of the situation—and he reminds Job that the God he's dealing with is much bigger than any struggle he will ever face. The omnipotent God quiets any questions Job, his three friends, or any of us dare to pitch to him. He meets Job—and us—right in the midst of the storm.

As we read God's response to Job in chapters 38–41, we see him reminding Job how big he is. He reveals his power through

- his ability to form all creation;
- his ability to oversee all creation; and
- his ability to subdue all creation.

At the end of the book, Job gets his fortunes restored, and God gives him more than he had the first time around. But when it comes down to it, that's not really the point. We must not misinterpret the final chapter of Job to mean that every trial will end with all our problems solved, all hard feelings forgiven, and everybody living happily ever after. It just doesn't always happen that way. The bigger purpose of the book's ending is to assure us that, no matter what happens, God always writes the last chapter. Therefore, we don't have to be afraid. We can trust God to do what is right, no matter how painful our situation may be.

YOU ARE NAMED BY GOD: *You are secure.*

CHAPTER 6

What's Love Got to Do with It?

GROWING UP IN A CHRISTIAN HOME and community, I thought I was on top of things when it came to being a "good girl." But sadly I had no concept of what it meant to have true transformation of the heart. In a twisted way, being "good" actually made it easier for me to mask the anger that was lurking in the depths of my heart. There were plenty of good-girl activities for me to participate in during the daytime hours that would make me feel better about what took place after dark.

As I think back now, I am disgusted by the hypocrisy in my life. During my teen years, a normal day would look something like this: singing my heart out at a youth choir rehearsal in the afternoon, then sneaking out after dark to some boy's house to try to fill my "need tank," which desperately craved worth and affection. After a few years of faking it to everyone around me, the charade became my reality. I kept thinking that if I was ever going to change, God would have to change my environment or get me out of my situation. But based on my experiences, I've found that God doesn't usually perform his miracles of transformation from the outside. This, dear one, is why you and I must take a healthy look into the mirror of our past, for he tends to work from the inside out.

I despair at the thought of blessings, opportunities, and victories I completely missed due to my stubbornness. I had given the Lord many pieces of my life as a teenager—the friends I hung out with, the way I talked, the way I dressed, my academics, almost everything you could see on the outside. However, I refused to give over the one part of me that God truly wanted: my whole heart. Every time I stuck my finger down my throat after a meal, every time I sliced the flesh on my forearm until I drew blood, every time I had a sexual encounter with a boy—all these were only symptoms of my disease. Every part of me was crying out for unconditional love, and God kept offering it to me. But I kept choosing my own way instead.

Maybe you can relate. Perhaps you think God's love is for other people, not for you. For many of you, this is the part where you're saying, "But, Kasey, you just don't understand! You don't know what he did to me; you don't know how she hurt me." And to you I say, "You're right. I don't understand." My beloved reader, I would never pretend to know your unique situation. For those of you who were abused as a child, I cannot imagine the anguish. For those of you who have experienced the death of a child, I cannot fathom the despair. For those of you who are struggling with a drug addiction or chemical dependency, I cannot comprehend the ache that such bondage brings. Although every human living on this planet shares the common bond of having a past, and although we can empathize with one another's pain, no one else will ever completely understand the intricate details of *your* story—your hurt, your sorrow, your pain, your trauma, your heartache, your weaknesses, your struggles.

But here is the beautiful part—they don't have to!

There is one who is capable of understanding the depths of who you are and what you've been through. He is the one who took every piece of your past—that wrong done against you, that individual who forced you to be a victim, that heartbreak so deep you didn't know if you'd live through it, that decision you made that carries with it excruciating pain and guilt—all of it. And he loves you. Completely. Unconditionally.

God's love is so much more than human love—the Bible describes it as a "love that surpasses knowledge" (Ephesians 3:19, NIV). To be loved by Jesus Christ is an indescribable thing, deeper than any of us can grasp or understand. God's love is not a product of what we do or don't do; it is not based on anything we can do for him. God's love is so pure and untainted that it cannot and will not allow us to continue in sin. The love of God means that God does whatever needs to be done, at any cost to himself or to us, to ensure that we will experience and be satisfied by his love forever.

My Mountaintop Moment

After four years of going my own way and rejecting God, he saw fit to reveal the bigger picture of his love to me. The Lord showed me a love that welcomed me unconditionally but also refused to tolerate sin. It all happened on a mountaintop in New Mexico when I was eighteen.

A shiver runs down my spine as I think back to that week at church camp. It was a week full of hypocrisy at its finest. Each day I woke up earlier than all the other girls in the bunkhouse to make sure my "natural" camp makeup was flawless and my sporty camp attire matched perfectly, from my headband to my Nikes. Each day I also planned my schedule carefully so I could follow Mark, a good Christian boy I had my scope set on.

I desperately wanted Mark to view me like the other good girls. I longed for him to see me the way I wanted to see myself—as someone worthy of his time and attention. And yet five grueling days later, and on the brink of exhaustion from all the acting I had been doing, I still had nothing to show for my efforts. Mark had yet to even acknowledge me, much less *speak* to me! And now we had reached the end of the week. Some sun-kissed, Scripture-quoting college girl was dragging my group up to the top of a mountain at ten o'clock at night to "talk about our feelings." *Give me a break!* I thought to myself.

God's love is so pure and untainted that it cannot and will not allow us to continue in sin.

The nine other girls and I gathered hesitantly in a circle around the fire as the spunky camp counselor managed to yell-whisper, "Okay, girls, I would like for us to go around the circle and each one tell how the Lord has spoken to you this week at camp." An immediate wave of steaming-hot terror rushed over me, and it was not from the fire that crackled inches away from my face.

One by one each girl spoke, but I could not for the life of me make out what they were saying. All I could think about was me—what in the world would I do when it was my turn? Only one girl was left before me, and I could feel my throat clamping shut. And then—silence. No one was talking anymore. In fact, everyone was staring at me! I thought to myself, *What now, Kasey? Come on, think of something! You're a good actress—make something up, for pity's sake! Tell them anything about God, quote John 3:16 or something—just don't break down. Don't tell them what's really on your heart. Then you would be the freak for admitting you came here for a guy, and none of these good, undamaged girls would understand.*

I never did come up with anything profound and "Christlike" to say. Instead, I began to cry. The tears started slowly at first, stinging my cheeks like tiny ant bites, then growing into full-fledged sobs. I couldn't bear to face the gaze of my shocked fellow campers, who all sat speechless, staring at me.

I don't know how to fully explain it, but that night my entire life changed. Beneath the polished, color-coordinated shell of an eighteen-year-old girl lurked seeping, open wounds. Not scars, not scar tissue, but gaping lesions of fear, insecurity, doubt, hurt, and anger. These wounds had been festering and getting deeper with each act of self-abuse, each experience of rejection, each unfulfilled longing to hear the words *I love you.*

There, upon that mountaintop, when I least expected it, I was finally broken. I'm not sure how much time passed before the hesitant college counselor pulled me aside. As we made our way toward a massive boulder that had perched itself along the mountain ledge in the middle of a clearing, my sobs subsided long enough for me to make out bits and pieces of the gentle prayer being whispered by the young woman.

This may seem like a cliché venue for my "come to Jesus" meeting, but that's exactly what happened. I came back to him. It was as if he were in the air that night, and I began to inhale him with gulps of remorse and sorrow, but also joy and triumph. I felt like I was intoxicated by his Spirit once again, and I could not get enough of him. In my brokenness and my repetitious ramblings to the effect of, "I'm sorry, please forgive me, I surrender," he released me from the chains of my guilty conscience and my anger. He forgave me and cleansed me of my sin, and he instilled a renewed sense of excitement to serve him. For the first time I was beginning to understand what true love was.

In a voice as mighty and clear as my feeble heart could comprehend, the Lord spoke to me atop that mountain: "Kasey, I have more for you, my child—more than you can begin to think or imagine. You will one day be my voice to the broken ones, and I will go before you. But you must surrender all to me."

Learning to Love
The first thing I sensed God calling me to do after I returned from my mountaintop experience was to take the love he'd given me and extend it to others. If I was going to be able to serve him at all, I had to let go of the anger from my past and forgive those who had hurt me.

So what's love got to do with it?

Everything!

Without love, it is impossible to move on. Without love, it is impossible to let go of anger and hurt. Without love, it is impossible to heal from the wounds of the past.

The moment I slammed my bags into the doorway of our home when I returned, I sprinted into my mother's room and asked her to forgive me for my disrespect and rebellion. I did the same with my father, and I released them both from my grasp of bitterness and rage. I told my mom the details of the night I was raped, and in my own heart, I released that young man from the clutches of my hatred and unforgiveness as well. I vowed to never again live in need of his apology, and I have stuck to that.

After returning home, I quickly discovered that loving others doesn't always feel like a mountaintop experi-ence. Unlike the feelings of love and mercy that washed over me when the Lord met me atop the mountain, I had moments when I felt absolutely no love toward my family or the young man who had betrayed me. But (and this is a big *but*) I had a fresh desire to know, love, and serve my Lord. I knew that as long as hatred remained in my heart, my relationship with the God I loved would be hindered. So as much as I detested the thought, as desperately as my flesh fought it, as constantly as Satan tried to sling that resentment back into my path to make me trip over it once again, I made the choice to love. Day after day, moment by moment, I chose forgiveness instead of bitterness, freedom instead of bond-age, love instead of hatred.

> Loving others doesn't always feel like a mountaintop experience.

One thing I learned early in my journey toward love is that I couldn't do it all on my own. For a time the process of learning to love felt like walking through the world blindfolded, arms waving frantically in front of me, terrified of what I might bump into. I needed divine help. So every day I got up, sought guid-ance from my Counselor, and trusted him to equip me with the love I needed to give away. If I ever wondered what real love looks like, I only needed to look at the one who took my bagful of hurt, anger, and bitterness, strapped it to his aching shoulders, and carried it up a hill. As he hung on the cross, it was the weight of my baggage that pulled excruciatingly at his nail-pierced hands and feet. He himself was guilty of no sin. No hatred had consumed him. And yet he was the one chosen by God to bear a burden that I deserved.

If you are attempting to give and receive love all on your own, please allow me to help pull that tremendous burden off your back, because it is never going to work! The Holy Spirit is the only channel through which real love can be produced. "If you love me, keep my commands. And I will ask the Father, and he will give you another advocate to help you and be with you forever— the Spirit of truth. The world cannot accept him, because it neither sees him nor knows him. But you know him, for he lives with you and will be in you" (John 14:15-17, NIV).

If you continue to act in the truth, the feeling will eventually come.

Years ago, when I was struggling to forgive and love, I reached out to an older woman in my church whom I greatly admired and respected. I didn't know much about her except that when I was in her presence, she radiated the peace of Jesus. I was terrified to confide in a family member or friend about my struggles to let go of deeply embedded bitterness, so I asked her to have lunch with me once a week. As we sat over our deli sandwiches and I finally got quiet from my venting, she said this to me, and it hit me like a bucket of ice water in my face. "In every situation life throws at you," she said, "react in truth. Although the feeling may not be there at first, if you continue to act in the truth, the feeling will eventually come." As she continued to sip her Diet Coke as if nothing profound had just happened, I nearly stopped breathing.

Over and over in my head I kept repeating, *So that means I don't have to feel like loving to love?*

This fundamental truth changed my life, as I pray it does for you. When we embrace this way of interacting with others, it will revolutionize every relationship. You may not feel loving toward your husband, but if you choose to love him despite his faults, you won't go through with that divorce. You may not feel like forgiving the person who betrayed you, but if you choose to act in love first, the feeling of release and forgiveness will eventually come. You may not feel worthy to receive the Lord's blessing and anointing on your life, but if you choose to accept his grace and redemption, you will eventually gain the confidence to go forward in your calling.

We will never be able to fully function while clinging to any pieces of our past. Call on the supernatural power of the Holy Spirit to give you the strength, and believe in the one who doesn't just understand love but *is* love.

> YOU ARE NAMED BY GOD: *You are his beloved.*

CHAPTER 7

The Healing Power
of Letting Go

IMAGINE WITH ME FOR A FEW MOMENTS. Let's say you're in the kitchen cutting up some veggies in preparation for the evening meal. The phone rings and startles you, and before your brain has a chance to transmit to your body that you are in pain, your eyes tell you that you've just cut your finger!

No one is around to help, so you run into the bathroom, turn on the faucet, and allow the fresh water to wash away the blood so you can get a better look. Yep, just as you had assumed, it looks pretty bad. But wait—you've got to finish cooking dinner! You wrap your finger in a towel, apply pressure to stop the bleeding, and return to the kitchen. But as soon as you start stirring the skillet on the stove, a dark spot begins to emerge on the towel. You shuffle frantically through the medicine cabinet for the Band-Aids. You apply one—no, *two*—Band-Aids on the cut. Surely this will let you get back to the pressing task of feeding your family. But soon the Band-Aids are soaked through, and the pain is now causing throbbing in your hand.

Your next attempt is to elevate your hand, wrap the towel around your finger *again*, and pace around, unsure of what to do next. Your kids are outside playing, your husband has yet to arrive home from work, and tears of pain are now beginning to fill your eyes. Sure, you could go to the doctor, but how silly would you feel if you loaded up your kids and had your hubby meet you at the doctor's office only for the good doctor to wrap your finger in some gauze and send you right back home? Besides, you're tough—you're a mom! You can take care of this yourself! You simply *must* get dinner cooked—the water is boiling over, and the oven is beeping frantically, telling you that your preheat is complete. This inconvenience will have to wait until later.

You march yourself back into the kitchen, wipe the tears from your eyes, and attempt to pick up the knife once more with your towel-wrapped hand. "Ouch!" You drop the knife. The towel is now completely soaked with blood, and the pain is almost unbearable. You know you should lay down your pride, load up the kids, and make your way to the doctor's office, but you just can't see taking the time to do that. Besides, if the doctor called for stitches, you'd have to give up your entire evening. If only the Band-Aid would work, you could have dinner on the table in no time.

This scenario might sound crazy, but it's exactly what we tend to do with areas of hurt from our past. We walk around, bleeding through our Band-Aids, waiting for a small piece of plastic to fix what's wrong. Meanwhile, the unending throb gets worse instead of better, and still we refuse the stitches needed to bring healing. The cut is much deeper than we ever realized—and deeper than we would admit to anyone, ourselves included.

The treatment for the wounds of our past may be inconvenient and even painful, but we will never truly heal unless we present our hurt to the Lord and trust him to do his work.

One Step at a Time

Step 1: Let God into your hurt

The first step toward healing is to be real with yourself and where you are in your hurt. You cannot sugarcoat your pain or pretend it's not there. Be honest with yourself and with God about your struggles. Don't be embarrassed or ashamed to verbalize exactly what emotions you are experiencing toward a person or a situation you've been hurt by. Remember, he already knows what happened to you, and he knows how it has affected you. But he wants you to bring it to him (see Hebrews 4:15-16). The first step toward home is asking your heavenly Father for directions. Admit that you took a wrong turn, that you are lost, and that you need some help making your way back.

God wants all of you—your pain included.

What I learned on that mountaintop in New Mexico at the age of eighteen was that God wanted all of me—my pain included. I had allowed God access to parts of my heart before, but that was the first time I had allowed God into my place of suffering.

Later that night, as the other girls crept into their bunk beds giggling, I was overcome with a silent sense of peace for the first time in my life. To say a huge weight had been lifted from my soul is a major understatement, but it's the closest I can come to explaining the almost physical relief that washed over me that night.

I was not completely healed and whole in that moment (as my later pitfalls into sin would testify), but I was most assuredly changed. I had let God into the deeper layers of my core that I had been withholding from him for years. His grace and forgiveness bathed over my life, and for the first time, I really believed it was true. Of course, I still had questions, but now everything looked different. My desire to follow the Lord overshadowed any lingering doubts and questions.

Step 2: Identify with Christ in his suffering

If you are willing to be real about your suffering before God, you won't necessarily find that your pain disappears, but you will find that it has a purpose. And you will find that you have the great privilege of identifying with the suffering Christ himself endured. Sometimes it's easy to believe that the pain you are experiencing is the ultimate pain, that no one can know the extent of the hurt you're enduring. You might think, *No one knows how bad this hurts* or *Other people have it much easier than I do.* But when you take your pain to God, your eyes begin to open to the reality of the agony Christ endured. Instead of comparing your pain with other people's pain, you can compare your suffering with what Christ experienced on the cross. And let's be honest here—our pain is just a drop in the bucket compared to what our Savior suffered.

Please understand: that doesn't mean God downplays or minimizes your hurt, and I'm not attempting to do that either. But in order to move past this place of agony, we must realize that the ultimate suffering has already been endured. And even more sobering, he experienced this suffering *for you*. It brings shivers down my spine to realize that the suffering taken on by the sinless Christ was done to take on *my* sin, to bear the burden of *my* suffering.

Humbly place your pain at the foot of the cross. Allow the blood from the wounds of Jesus to drip all over it until it is covered, until you can no longer see it. Then look up into his bruised and bleeding face as he struggles for breath from the weight of his collapsing lungs. Look into the eyes of the "man of sorrows" (Isaiah 53:3, KJV). Isaiah prophesied that the people of Israel would hear Jesus and see Jesus, and yet refuse to believe he was the true Messiah they longed for. In Jesus' lifetime he was despised, looked down upon, and rejected by the very ones he came to save. From that perspective, our sorrow becomes little more than a faint shadow in the distance, paling in comparison to the suffering of the innocent Lamb of God.

Step 3: Trust that God will bring justice to your pain

Okay, you're heading home. Keep your eyes fixed on the front door! I pray that you have been real with God about your hurt. I pray that you have taken your pain before him and been humbled by his suffering. Now it's time to deal with that fleshly part of you that keeps seeking revenge—that human desire that says, "I want payback! I want the person who hurt me to get what he has coming to him. I want to see my name avenged!"

Believe me, I understand the feeling. I spent years wanting the person who caused me pain to be hurt in return. Maybe you're there right now. You don't want those who wounded you to prosper; you don't want them to succeed in their work; you don't want them to be accepted by a church body; you don't want them to be loved by anyone, for that matter. You know your pain doesn't compare to Christ's, but you still feel entitled to roll your eyes or think a spiteful thought every time you hear the name of that person who hurt you.

You might as well know this up front: I'm a fighter. When I was a child, my mom and dad were convinced I would become a lawyer when I grew up. They would always say, "Kasey, you'd pick a fight with that *wall* over there. And the crazy thing is—you'd win!" From the time I was very young, I had the consuming urge to defend myself and my opinion at every opportunity.

Letting go is the only way to be free from the grip of bitterness in your life.

Now, as an adult, I face similar battles daily as I fight the urge to justify myself. You can ask my husband—I even go so far as to justify why I burned the chicken! (There's no justification for the burned chicken, by the way. I'm just not a good cook, and I burned it. The end.)

The difficult truth about this broken world, however, is that as much as we crave justice, we often will never see wrongs made right in our lifetime. I have never heard, nor do I ever expect to hear, an acknowledgment, much less an apology, from the young man who raped me. But the brilliant truth is, I no longer need it to be able to move on and find healing.

This life-changing morsel of truth did not come easily for me, nor did it come overnight. It was a gradual process for me to give up my "right" to see that wrong justified, to exact revenge on the one who hurt me. As God began prying my fingers off my need for justice, these lessons went down as pleasantly as a spoonful of castor oil! But letting go was the only way I could be free from the grip of bitterness in my life. As long as I held on to my need for an "I'm sorry," I was the one being wrung through the wringer, not him. As long as I was holding out for an apology, I was pulling further and further away from God's blessing in my life. Eventually, after a long time of wrestling over what had been done to me, I felt God clearly speak this truth into my spirit: "Kasey, forgiveness has nothing to do with your response to him and everything to do with your response to me."

It isn't that God doesn't care about justice; it's that it isn't up to me to carry it out. I need to trust that he'll do what is right and fair . . . without my help. "God is just: He will pay back trouble to those who trouble you and give relief to you who are troubled" (2 Thessalonians 1:6-7, NIV). These verses remind us that one day everyone will stand before God. At that time, all wrongs will be righted by God—the only one who is completely just.

When we desire to carry out justice against another person, we are, in essence, claiming to be someone we're not: God!

Step 4: Love your enemy

If you are as human as I am, this step of loving your enemy probably seems over the line. This might be the point where you're thinking, *Okay, God, come on! I've done some really difficult things already here—like entrusting my hurt to you and letting go of my desire for justice on my own terms. Now you're telling me to love my enemy?* It just seems like too much to ask. But Jesus doesn't mince words when he gives us this mind-boggling command: "If you love those who love you, what credit is that to you? Even sinners love those who love them. . . . But love your enemies, do good to them, and lend to them without expecting to get anything back. Then your reward will be great, and you will be children of the Most High" (Luke 6:32, 35, NIV).

Before we can really talk about what it means to love our enemies, though, we need to adjust our definition of what love is. We tend to view love from a human perspective, rather than from a heavenly one. When Christ refers to loving our enemies, he isn't talking about a feeling. He doesn't mean the kind of love you "fall into" with that guy you've had a crush on for months. The genuine love he's talking about is an act of the will. It is a conscious effort to act in the best interest of others—even those who have hurt us.

Does this task sound unbearable to you? Does it sound like too much for God to ask? The good news is that this love is not something we have to conjure up out of our own emotions or resources. It's something that comes from the God who is himself love (see 1 John 4:8). He loves us when we are unlovable and when we act in direct defiance to him. No matter how we treat him, he continues to forgive us, love us, and act in our best interest. That's the kind of love we have access to—the love he asks us to give others as well.

A few years ago I engaged in a difficult but much-needed conversation with a woman who had once been my close friend. However, when our personal symptoms of deeply rooted sin (namely, pride) rose to the surface and collided, it wasn't pretty. We called a momentary truce one summer afternoon in order to attempt reconciliation. I'll spare you the gory details, but suffice it to say the conversation did not end as I had hoped—certainly not in reconciliation. Just as we were parting ways, my former friend finally uttered, "I have forgiven you . . . but I do *not* love you!"

For a time I clung to this statement as a glimmer of hope. Obviously we were not over everything that had gone down, but it seemed that restoration might be possible if she was willing to forgive me. I should have known better, though, because true forgiveness is impossible without love. As much as I am sure this woman intended to forgive me, she had reversed the biblical steps required to do so, meaning there was no genuine forgiveness.

In 1 Corinthians 13, Paul makes a bold statement about love: "If I could speak all the languages of earth and of angels, but didn't love others, I would only be a noisy gong or a clanging cymbal. If I had the gift of prophecy, and if I understood all of God's secret plans and possessed all knowledge, and if I had such faith that I could move mountains, but didn't love others, I would be nothing" (verses 1-2). Without love, we are incapable of channeling the supernatural power of God's Spirit within us.

Perhaps one of the greatest human misconceptions is that it's possible to forgive another person prior to extending love to him or her. The hard truth is that if you desire authentic healing and a God-honoring lifestyle, you must choose to forgive in the same way our Lord does—by extending love first.

Step 5: Forgive the one who hurt you

Oh no, there's that word again! You know, the word that makes you cringe whenever you read about it. The word that makes you sink a little lower in your seat at church when your pastor preaches about it. The word you have been avoiding for some time now because you think that one day things will just magically get better. It's that beautiful but gut-wrenching word—*forgiveness*.

Before we can understand how to forgive, we need to come to an accurate working definition. At its core, forgiveness is an act of pardon—acknowledging the hurt that has been done but not demanding that the offender pay for what he has done. Forgiving means releasing the other person from the clutches of your thoughts and feelings. This doesn't mean you have to forget the past offense, but it does mean you no longer continue to dwell on it.

Forgiveness originated with God and was created by God. Hebrews 9:22 states, "Without the shedding of blood, there is no forgiveness." Blood is our life source. It is how we live and breathe. Under the old covenant, one of the ways people and objects were made acceptable before the Lord was by purifying them with blood (see Exodus 30:10). In order for sin to be forgiven, blood must first be shed.

When Jesus shed his blood for us on the cross, he in turn gave us his breath, his very life, as a payment for our sins. In doing so, he set the ultimate example of forgiveness. The spilling of Jesus' blood not only represents the new covenant for believers today but also purifies us as acceptable before a holy God.

As humans, we like to set a "sin scale" in order to justify our own behavior. We want to stand in judgment of the person who has committed murder, but we have no problem spending all day gabbing on the phone with our girlfriends, spreading rumors and causing dissension in relationships. It's time for a reality check, my friend: Jesus Christ was nailed to the cross for *all* sin! He bled and died for the "not that bad," the "pretty bad," and the "really bad."

If you find yourself tempted to categorize a particular sin in your life or in the lives of others, or if you find it difficult to believe that God has called you to forgive, allow Matthew 6:14-15 to hit your face like a bucket of cold water: "If you forgive other people when they sin against you, your heavenly Father will also forgive you. But if you do not forgive others their sins, your Father will not forgive your sins" (NIV). When you withhold forgiveness from another person, you are taking for granted the precious blood of Christ, as well as disqualifying yourself from being the recipient of his forgiveness.

> Forgiving means releasing the other person from the clutches of your thoughts and feelings.

For most of us, it is easy to ask God to forgive us . . . yet difficult for us to grant forgiveness to others. Jesus' words in Matthew are a startling reminder that when we refuse to forgive others, we are denying our common ground as sinners. We are dismissing the fact that we are just as in need of forgiveness as the person who hurt us.

If there is someone you are struggling to forgive, it might make you feel better to know that even the disciples had a difficult time comprehending this concept. In the book of Matthew, we read about Peter's conversation with Jesus about forgiveness. He asks, "Lord, how often should I forgive someone who sins against me? Seven times?" For anyone who has ever been hurt, Jesus' reply is nothing short of shocking: "No, not seven times . . . but seventy times seven!" (18:21-22).

Peter probably thought he was being pretty loving and generous with his offer of forgiving seven times. But when the Lord responds with, "Uh, no, Peter—try 490 times," I picture Peter tripping backward over his own lack of faith.

The point here is not the literal number, because in all honesty you may be called to forgive more than that over the course of a lifetime. The point Jesus is making here is that forgiveness is a process, with no limits or dimensions. Since love "keeps no record of being wronged" (1 Corinthians 13:5), by the time we have learned to forgive our brothers and sisters that many times, we will be in the habit of forgiving.

If you are struggling to forgive someone for a past hurt, I strongly encourage you to seek godly counsel as you navigate this difficult process. Depending on the situation, it may be appropriate to make amends or reconcile with the offender. There can be an extra layer of healing that takes place when we forgive someone in our hearts and then go to that person and tell him or her. In some cases, especially if reconnecting with the offender would put you in harm's way, it may not be appropriate to try to restore the relationship. In these situations, a letter or communication through a mediator may suffice. But no matter what your specific situation looks like, God calls you to release the other person from that heavy burden . . . and to extend love and forgiveness instead.

Step 6: Cry out for power

In order to complete the last step in our healing process, we must cry out for power directly from God. We are fooling ourselves if we believe we are capable of extending this kind of forgiveness and love through our own strength. But God gives us *his* power through the Holy Spirit: "Since we live by the Spirit, let us keep in step with the Spirit" (Galatians 5:25, NIV).

If we're attempting to love and forgive another person by sheer determination on our part, we will only end up wasting enormous amounts of sideways energy. Even if we have the best of intentions, they will be for nothing if we attempt forgiveness apart from Christ's supernatural power.

When Paul tells us to "keep in step with the Spirit," he is essentially saying that we need to make sure our daily lives are under the control and direction of God, and not the flesh. So then, what is the access code to this power from the Lord?

> Let us go right into the presence of God with sincere hearts fully trusting him. For our guilty consciences have been sprinkled with Christ's blood to make us clean, and our bodies have been washed with pure water. Let us hold tightly without wavering to the hope we affirm, for God can be trusted to keep his promise. HEBREWS 10:22-23

Because of Christ's sacrifice on the cross, we have direct access to God! By pursuing him daily through Scripture, prayer, and service, we can live victoriously in his power.

• • •

You have reached the threshold of your home. Are you ready to turn the doorknob and walk humbly into the healing embrace of your Father? As we come to the end of this chapter, are you calling on Christ's healing power over every ounce of pain and suffering in your life, or are you stubbornly hanging on to the pain?

Let it go from your grasp, dear one.

As long as you cling to your pain, you are allowing another person's sin to dominate you and have power over you. That means you are stuck continually in the role of the victim. Do not take for granted the blood that was shed on the cross for you! Drop your pain on the front steps of the porch, and walk through the door. I'd be honored to be the first one to welcome you home.

YOU ARE NAMED BY GOD: *You are filled with his power.*

Part 2

Transforming Your Present

THIS PAST WINTER my family took a vacation to the mountains to learn how to snow ski. Because my husband had never skied before and I had tried it only once in high school, we figured now was as good a time as ever to cross another item off the old bucket list.

As Justin and I headed toward the bottom of the slopes to sign up for our first day of ski school, I noticed a rather cool-looking group of individuals gathered around a cool-looking young man who was giving instructions—not on how to ski, but on how to snowboard. I immediately made my way to a spot where I could overhear the instructor. After five minutes of eavesdropping, I had fully determined that snowboarding seemed much more my thing than plain old skiing. (Is it obvious that I was going through a "just turned thirty" crisis?)

My husband, not yet knowing the difference, agreed to take

the snowboarding lesson with me, and off we went to feel younger than we truly were. And boy, did we look the part—complete with our neon pink and green snowboards. No dorky ski poles for us! We were completely free to glide down the mountain atop a mini surfboard. That was cool.

But actually *learning* to snowboard . . . well, that was *not* so cool!

Day one wasn't so bad. I made it up and off the ski lift successfully, although getting down the bunny slope was a bit more challenging. I mostly face-planted my way down, but I was confident the next day would be an improvement.

On day two I was sore but still determined. At one point Justin and I collided into each other so hard that he cracked his rib, but still I refused to give up! I spent the entire day mastering the . . . wait for it . . . bunny slope. Sure, it took me an hour to make it twenty feet, but hey, I stayed upright for the entire time.

When we hit day three, I was beginning to wonder how the word *vacation* fit into this scenario at all. I awoke to day three no longer feeling cool . . . just old. My mind was still in the game, but my body was still in the bed. Every joint and muscle I had (including ones I didn't know I had) was begging me to take a break. But no, I was here to learn something new and prove to myself that I could do this. So although every step was excruciating, I made it back up (and down) the bunny slope for my day three warm-up.

Despite the fact that my knees were quivering beneath me, I determined that it was finally time for me to take my snowboarding up a notch—to a death-defying green hill! I stood at the top with both feet locked firmly in place on the board. From the bottom this hill had looked easy, but now that I was up here,

I was suddenly starting to panic. There was no way my throbbing muscles and shaking knees could make it down this thing! As skiers and boarders flew by me, I began to doubt everything about myself. My mind started running a loop of, *What were you thinking trying something like this? You are too old to learn something new! You will make it down all right, but only on the back of the paramedic's snowmobile!*

Much to my dismay, there was only one way off the mountain: down. So I took a deep breath, swallowed my pride, and took off down the mountain.

Yes, I fell down—many times. Yes, it took me forever to get to the bottom. Yes, people were whizzing past me. And yes, I was terrified the entire time. But to my utter surprise, I also had fun!

When I got to the bottom I had a bruise the size of Texas on my left hip, my head was spinning from too many encounters with the icy slope, and I had sprained my wrist. But I had done it! In spite of all the pain and drama, I had taken that mountain.

In many ways, part 2 of this book is like standing at the top of a daunting hill, strapped to your snowboard. You've done your training and dealt with the painful experiences of your past, and now it's time to try your hand at the mountain.

For many of us, this is the scary part. There are risks that come with change—the danger of failing at something new, of falling flat on our faces, of getting our pride wounded. And chances are, when we get to the top, the mountain will look much steeper than it did from the bottom. And most assuredly, others will be flying by, maybe even bumping into us, throughout the entire trek down. There will be moments when, with every inch of our being, we will want to stay frozen at the top.

But if you want to experience the thrill of letting God transform your present, at some point you have to get off the bunny slope. And remember, the only way to get down is to take the mountain for yourself!

CHAPTER 8

Looking in the Mirror

IN THE PREVIOUS SECTION WE TALKED about how past hurts can hold us back from the Lord's richest blessings. But now it's time to face an equally painful reality: taking responsibility for moments in the present when our own sin is the culprit for another person's pain.

One of the biggest roadblocks in our relationship with God is unacknowledged or unconfessed sin in our lives. God desires to unleash his power in us, but we prevent it from becoming a reality when we refuse to deal with our sin.

There are many factors that can keep us stuck in a cycle of sin: attacks from Satan, the distractions of a fallen world, or simply our own flesh, which tempts us to doubt God's good purpose for us. No matter the cause, the common factor is our lack of desire to change. We muddle our way through life because either we're unwilling to change or we feel it's impossible to make the changes God desires us to make. We say things like "I'm just not good at change" or "I'm too far gone to change now" or "I was just born this way—there's nothing I can do about it." These are all lies from the mouth of the deceiver, but we are quick to buy into them.

The truth, however, is that change is possible, no matter who you are or where you've been. In Genesis 4 we read the account of Cain and Abel, Adam and Eve's sons. Cain is most commonly remembered for murdering his brother, but the trouble begins before that, when he starts letting anger, bitterness, and jealousy consume him. In verse 7 the Lord tells Cain that although sin is "eager to control" him, Cain has the power to "subdue it and be its master." God is giving Cain the access code to living free from sin in his life and in healthy fellowship with his brother, but Cain chooses instead to give in to that sin.

> Change is possible, no matter who you are or where you've been.

Galatians 5:22-23 tells us that the Holy Spirit is the one who equips us with everything we need for total transformation. Whenever God requires something of us—holy living, godly actions and attitudes, a heart that is right before him—he gives us the power we need at every moment to pull it off. In other words—we have no excuse *not* to change!

As we look at our past, we must admit that the sinful patterns we witnessed as children can easily become a part of our personalities and actions in the present. We easily justify these habits, and sometimes we barely notice them leaking into our current behaviors. Almost unconsciously, we allow these sinful patterns to become second nature to us, blurring the line between truth and lies, between godliness and sin. The painful reality is that once we start to blur this line, we find ourselves becoming the very thing we detest in others—namely, a hurter.

In order to experience total transformation in our present, it is vital to understand up front just who we are fighting. Oh! Did you not realize we are at war? Well, friend, not only are we at war with the world and our flesh, but we also have a furious enemy coming straight toward us. If you don't know him very well, we've got a lot of work to do. Because I assure you, he has spent quite a bit of time getting to know *you*.

The Prince of the World

A precious teacher once told me, "If you cannot remember your most recent attack from Satan, then you might not be doing enough to catch his attention!" It took many years for that statement to sink into my thick brain. But the moment I found myself on the receiving end of a demonic arrow straight to the forehead, those words echoed loud and clear. If you are a passionate pursuer of Christ, it is not a question of *if* Satan will attack you but *when*. That leads us to the next question: when Satan attacks, will you be armed and ready for battle?

Before we go any further in this conversation, I would like to take a moment to clarify a few things about the character of Satan. It seems that people tend to err on one side or the other when it comes to our enemy. There are those who give Satan too much power . . . and those who do not give him enough. We don't need to live in fear, looking for a demon around every corner, but we also need to be aware that Satan is armed, dangerous, deceitful, and manipulative. He is *not*, however, equal to the Most High

God. The Lord is the Creator, and Satan is only a created being. Although Satan is a threat, he is no match for the omnipotent, sovereign God.

Now that we have a clearer picture of where Satan falls in relation to God, we need to take into account these facts: Satan is real, and he desires to destroy you. His desire is to turn you into the hurter you never intended to be. The battle is on, and we need to equip ourselves to fight. This is no ordinary battle, because we are fighting "against evil rulers and authorities of the unseen world, against mighty powers in this dark world, and against evil spirits in the heavenly places" (Ephesians 6:12). If we're going to be prepared to fight our enemy, we must know him and his strategy.

The Bible describes Satan as a prowling lion whose every intent is to devour us (see 1 Peter 5:8). John 8:44 says that Satan is a murderer and liar. One of the most common ways he tries to deceive us is by denying or distorting God's Word. As long as we're living in this world, we're going to have to be on our guard against these attacks from the devil, because according to 1 John 5:19, the whole world is under the control of the evil one.

I cringe and sink a little lower in my seat when I think back on the moments in my life when I have chosen to believe the enticing lies of Satan—the moments when I have allowed those lies to pull me further and further into a web of sin, the moments when I have found myself in complete and utter bondage to the evil one, so entangled I could hardly breathe, and the moment—*that* moment—when my disgusting, sinful state, so manipulated by the enemy, constructed and released a sharp arrow that wounded another human being.

Have you been there? Have you been the one on the other

end of the bow, pulling back on the strings, suddenly releasing your fingers and watching as the arrow pierced your target? If this scene is all too familiar to you, take heart as you read the following words.

One of the most merciful gifts God gives us is the rather uncomfortable gift of conviction. If you are a child of the King, at some point after your arrow was released, you raised your hands to your cheeks and gasped in horror at the sight of your dart hitting its mark. You might have cried something like "What have I done?" or "If I could only take it back . . ." or "Who is this person I have become?" For the believer, an attack—intentional or unintentional—against another person brings just as much pain into *your* life as it does to the one you hurt. But that sense of conviction is actually a good thing, because it's what God uses to bring you back to himself.

If you cannot remember your most recent attack from Satan, then you might not be doing enough to catch his attention!

If you are feeling trapped by the tactics of Satan, it's time to claim the protection that God has made available to us.

> Be strong in the Lord and in his mighty power. Put on all of God's armor so that you will be able to stand firm against all strategies of the devil. For we are not fighting against flesh-and-blood enemies, but against evil rulers and authorities of the unseen world, against mighty powers in this dark world, and against evil spirits in the heavenly places.
>
> Therefore, put on every piece of God's armor so you will be able to resist the enemy in the time of evil. Then after the battle

you will still be standing firm. Stand your ground, putting on the belt of truth and the body armor of God's righteousness. For shoes, put on the peace that comes from the Good News so that you will be fully prepared. In addition to all of these, hold up the shield of faith to stop the fiery arrows of the devil. Put on salvation as your helmet, and take the sword of the Spirit, which is the word of God.

Pray in the Spirit at all times and on every occasion. Stay alert and be persistent in your prayers for all believers everywhere. EPHESIANS 6:10-18

The belt of truth is not a weapon of offense, but of protection. As we memorize God's Word and grow in deeper knowledge of it, we have no guarantee that this will prevent an attack of Satan. But it will keep us from being harmed by his advances.

By covering our hearts with the breastplate of righteousness, we are protecting our feelings from the opinions and slander of others. When Satan attacks the precious organ of our hearts through other people's fiery darts, their words will not be able to penetrate our sense of acceptance from the Lord.

As we lace up our shoestrings of peace, we learn to walk with confidence against the attacks of Satan. The Christian soldier soon learns that the best war tactic is to fight with peace, not opposition.

Our shield of faith will not keep the enemy from throwing his darts, but it will most certainly prevent him from starting a fire in our lives. Faith is believing God is bigger than we have ever believed him to be, and bigger than any enemy we face.

The helmet of salvation wages war against the hopelessness, worry, and fear that tend to plague our minds. When our minds stay focused on the assurance of our salvation, as well as the inevitable return of Christ, we can keep our courage in the face of any opposition from Satan.

Although the other pieces of our armor are defensive, the sword of the Spirit works on the offense! Material swords get dull and ineffective the more they are used, but the spiritual sword of God (aka the Bible) only gets sharper and more precise with each use. If you find yourself trapped in the web of Satan, there is only one option: take out your sword and cut away the sticky strands that are holding you back.

The Battle of the Flesh

Satan is not the only enemy—we also fight against our own flesh. We were born with a fallen, sinful nature. Our default is to choose self over God and self over others, and our fleshly desires wreak havoc in our lives and our relationships.

As we seek to transform our present, we must unmask each weak and ugly area that dwells within us. We must allow God to bring change into every ounce of our marrow. I pray that we prepare our minds for "sincere and pure devotion to Christ" (2 Corinthians 11:3, NIV), no longer allowing ourselves to be led by our own flesh.

In Romans 7:15-25, Paul teaches us that as humans we consistently operate within one of two spheres: the law of sin, which is the flesh, or the law of the Spirit, which is Christ. When we become followers of Christ, our old sinful nature doesn't magically disappear. But in Christ, we are given a new nature. This new nature is the Holy Spirit indwelling our lives, and he has the power to crucify our old sinful nature every moment of every day.

This is why Christianity is a daily battle. Although we desire to live in obedience to Christ, our flesh is still present, tempting us in the opposite direction.

• • •

If you are entering this chapter at the bottom of a dark cavern of sin, it is time to look up into the clear blue sky of repentance. It is time to take hold of the hands reaching down to pull you out. No longer do you have to allow Satan to hurt you, and no longer does your own flesh have to hurt others. You can let God transform you and no longer remain a slave to your broken, wounded self. Wherever you are in life, I'd like to invite you to open your heart to God and let him reveal those broken areas to you as you reflect on my story.

When Sin Creeps In

We have come to a point of confession in my story. In the past thirty years I have been struck by many blows from Satan, and I've been tempted countless times by the weakness of my own flesh. I praise God for the moments I called on his mighty power and wisdom to fight back against those attacks. But I shamefully regret the times I found myself tangled in a web of sin spun by Satan or by my own sinful desires.

We've walked together quite a ways on this journey, and you, dear reader, now know as much about me as a treasured friend would. At this point in my story, I pray that you don't doubt my sincere and undying love for our Lord. As someone who has gone from walking upright one moment to lying face down in the dirt the next, I want you to know that I love my God with every inch of my being. But as I learned the hard way, loving God doesn't make us immune to sin or attacks by the enemy.

Throughout my journey of knowing what it means to be named by God, I have learned that there is risk involved in baring my most repulsive and nauseating scars. Sometimes we become so comfortable in our snug, cozy masks that we feel compelled to look away when other people remove theirs. Simply put, other people's messes are just too much for some of us to handle.

But even so, I feel compelled to share my story with you. In my years of Bible teaching, I've received hundreds of e-mails and letters from Christians who bear similar scars to my own. More and more I'm realizing that the majority of us, churchgoers included, bear a story that's not for the faint of heart. And along the way I've learned a brilliant and grace-filled truth: more people can relate to "messy" than they can to "pretty." Armed with that knowledge, I'm willing to risk having someone walk away from me after hearing about my journey if it means I can have the opportunity to help someone who is bearing a heavy burden. We are instructed in Galatians 6:2 to "share each other's burdens, and in this way obey the law of Christ," and that is what I hope to do in sharing my story with you.

I am willing to make myself vulnerable if it means someone else may get a taste of what I have experienced—proof that God is a loving, gracious God. That, my friend, is what I live for.

• • •

It was during one of the greatest seasons of growing and knowing my Lord that I became a prime target for Satan and his deceptive ways, and to my own desires of the flesh. And when the attacks came, this pitiful girl fell hard.

May I take a moment to officially introduce you to my man—my husband, Justin. I can hardly write his name without crying because I still feel so unworthy of this man and his love. God gave him to me around my twentieth birthday, and within a matter of a few weeks we were saying "I love you." We just knew. (Yeah, I know it sounds cliché.) He was (and is) wonderful, loving, and tender, and he had saved himself for marriage. We were oh so different, and yet oh so meant to be.

I was the loud, attention-seeking, adventuresome self-motivator. He was the laid-back, non-risk-taking love of my life. The day I laid bare all my dark secrets to him was not one I would ever choose to repeat, but it was also beautiful, as he readily extended to me the same grace, love, and forgiveness that God had already given to me.

After two years of dating, we were married in our home church, where we had met and fallen in love. Together we began taking on more responsibility within our church. We were young, passionate, and zealous to bring revival to our church and ultimately to our town. I would spend hours upon hours each week journaling my vision, writing devotions and study plans, researching church movements. I can see now that the Lord used this season to begin chiseling me into a teacher and a speaker. Although no one besides my husband seemed to understand the dream the Lord had given me on the New Mexico mountain, I knew in the depths of my soul that he had called me to be a messenger to the broken ones—I just had no idea when, where, or how exactly that would come to be. Nevertheless, I spent loads of time getting ready for it . . . whatever "it" would be.

As far as we fall, we will never fall further than the reach of our Savior.

I had received my bachelor's degree in both speech communication and psychology, and since I wasn't sure what to do in either field, I thought it would be wise to stay in school until I figured it out (although our bank account thought differently!). I was only one year into my master's program when it was figured out for me . . . with a positive pregnancy test!

Justin and I were ecstatic. I kept up with my studies, and with only three months to go before baby, I walked proudly across the stage to receive my MA in community counseling (and yes, I looked like an orca whale in the black gown).

As new parents in our mid-twenties, with no money, it would have been easy to get sidetracked from our vision of revival for our town. But God wouldn't let us drop it. We had a heart for young people, so alongside my small ministry team of college students from our home church, we figured the local college campus was a good place to start.

I laugh now when I think about my first excursion onto the campus. You see, the Lord instilled a "no fear" gene in me when it comes to sharing my faith. When pointed at the wrong thing, this can be devastating, but when it's the right thing at the right time, God can make it awe inspiring. Everyone stood around with jaws dropped as I attacked this thirty-five thousand–member campus without an ounce of trepidation. I approached complete strangers all afternoon, asking them what they thought of the town, the churches, and Jesus. The answers I received left me staggering. Almost every student I talked to was lost—completely and utterly lost. Some students were struggling with their sexual identity, some completely denied God's existence, some were cohabiting with their significant other, some were openly involved in drugs and orgies, some were involved in self-mutilation, and the list goes on. In a single moment, it was like a switch was flipped inside me. All my heart longed for was to have these lost people come to know that God had immeasurably more for them.

I couldn't eat, I couldn't sleep—all I could talk about for months were these beautiful, wandering souls. On my weekly afternoon visits to the campus, the Lord broke my heart for the unsaved of this world and clearly revealed to me that he wanted me to spend my life pursuing people who were far from him.

But also right around that time, it was as if something started to gradually shrivel up inside me. I don't know exactly why it happened or what factors caused it. Perhaps it was a sense of loneliness I felt in my passion for the lost, or maybe it was a feeling of bewilderment in not knowing what to do with the limited resources at my disposal. There was no sudden, single crisis moment that led to my discouragement—it was more of a slow disconnect between me and all that seemed right in the world. I call those four years of my life the desert years. With the exception of the glorious birth of my daughter in the middle of that season, those years were spiritually dry for me as the plague of sin gradually began to infest every part of me.

If you had been walking with me through those years, you might have assumed they were anything but dry. I was at church every time the doors opened. In fact, I was completely overcommitted, serving and taking part in every opportunity available. And here's where it happened—I suddenly became so involved in ministry that I completely missed God. I was so bent on a personal course to be a good Christian that I missed his plan for me, inadvertently scribbling out my own plan for my life and future.

You want to know the problem? Well, I said it six times in the last paragraph: *I*. One little letter that can cause a whole heap of destruction in a well-intentioned Christian's life. What I know now is that Satan was not that concerned if I had a dream to change the world. He wasn't really worried when I showed up for church or busied myself in a multitude of ministries. And he didn't even get ruffled when, on my own power, I did my best to read my Bible and obey the Ten Commandments.

I didn't realize it at the time, but Satan knew all my buttons and just when and how to push them. He knew what made me tick, what made me angry, what made me hungry, what made me passionate, what made me discouraged, and certainly what made me act in a way that was completely motivated by self. Even if I looked good from the outside, he knew where my armor was weak. He took one of the most ministry-focused seasons of my life, knowing that my eyes were fixed on *my* vision instead of the Lord's, and he threw me a curveball that I never saw coming.

I thought something like this could never happen to a girl like me, and that's exactly where Satan needed me. With just enough pride to believe I couldn't fall and just enough insecurity from my past tucked away in my back pocket, I fell. And I fell hard.

But praise God—as far as we fall, we will never fall further than the reach of our Savior. My life is proof that the Lord loves us when we are at our most wretched, and he lavishes his mercy on us when we least deserve it. He knew I would choose this awful path long before I did, and he made sure the blood of his Son would cover it before it even happened. I find great comfort in these words from Scripture:

He was merciful and forgave their sins and did not destroy them all. Many times he held back his anger and did not unleash his fury! PSALM 78:38

He has rescued us from the kingdom of darkness and transferred us into the Kingdom of his dear Son, who purchased our freedom and forgave our sins.

COLOSSIANS 1:13-14

YOU ARE NAMED BY GOD: *You are forgiven.*

CHAPTER 9

Waking Up

I'VE HEARD MANY MARRIED COUPLES CONFESS that their first year of marriage was the most difficult time of adjustment for them. But for my man and me, it was the year after *baby* that hit us like a sucker punch to the gut.

Somewhere amid career callings, the construction of a home, a sink full of baby bottles, a gazillion loads of laundry, and trash bags full of dirty diapers, the young couple who had once spent hours talking on the phone just to hear the sound of the other person's breathing soon transformed into two very different people, going very different directions. He was the insurance salesman who paid the bills, played with the baby every moment he was home, faithfully took out the trash, and crashed in the recliner no later than eight o'clock. She was the cleaner, decorator, cook, and bottle-making mom who cried every day as she stood in the middle of a four-foot pile of dirty laundry and crashed by nine o'clock, only to wake up three hours later to feed a crying baby.

After countless sleepless nights, several unpaid hospital bills, and months of my postpartum depression chased with a prescription for Xanax, Justin and I woke up one day not sure what had happened to the people who had said, "I do," at the altar only a few years before. Please don't misunderstand; we still loved each other, but we no longer liked who we were—as individuals or as a couple.

Having a baby—and all the extras that came with it—soon distracted us from pursuing each other. Somewhere along the way, Justin and I had forgotten that a marriage means waking up each day and choosing to love the other person, even when you don't feel like it. The pieces of our personality that had once made us balance each other so well now seemed to be working against us and drawing us further apart.

The stress and pressure of providing for a growing family zapped Justin of the energy he had left for our daughter and me. By the time he returned home after a hard day at the office, he had already used up his words and his desire to be a leader. He had been talking, making decisions, and pursuing people all day, and by five o'clock, he was done.

But for me, five o'clock was when I needed him most! I had been conversing with a six-month-old all day, amid spit-up, poop, and foul-smelling formula bottles, and I was finally ready for some adult conversation. I had not been out of my flannel pajamas, nor felt any resemblance to being a sexy woman, since the birth of our daughter, and by five o'clock, I needed to feel wanted and pretty again.

As weeks turned into months, my husband and I felt more and more like the proverbial "ships passing in the night." It also seemed as if all my dreams, visions, and plans for my future as God's messenger were overshadowed by a tiny person who always, *always* needed me! And the man who at one time thrilled at my touch was now too tired to need me.

I spiraled into depression. Medication just numbed the ache and kept me from crying so much. With each passing week of missed quiet times with the Lord, church services where I merely went through the motions, and evenings spent in front of the television with no meaningful conversation, I struggled to find a resemblance to the life I'd envisioned for myself. Soon I began to feel the familiar pull of a boarded-up old "friend"—insecurity.

The Stench of Sin

The longing for validation began as an ache at first, like an annoying splinter in the tip of my finger. But it didn't take long for it to start throbbing like a full-blown infection racing up my arm. On the outside I was holding it together—my words easily deceived those closest to me (even Justin) into believing I was a happy, healthy individual. I even fooled myself into thinking I was strong enough to handle my pain myself and keep it hidden deep inside.

That was precisely the opening Satan seized in his full-fledged assault against me. He fed me the lie that I could be just enough "god" in my life to meet my needs without getting hurt—and without hurting anyone else around me. And so, to my shame, I began to turn to a man who was not my husband to fill the void inside me.

For three years I jumped in and out of the web of infidelity, completely under the radar of those closest to me. For three years I ran back and forth between God's purpose for me and Satan's plans for my demise. What first looked like a fantasy world soon became Satan's trap, and before I knew it I found myself in full-blown bondage. Yet I still tried to keep up the charade while maintaining my reputation as a good church girl.

However, as I mentioned earlier, the Lord does not allow his children to keep sinning successfully. Mercifully, the rot of my sin began to affect me mentally, emotionally, and physically, and God brought me to a place of being completely wrecked by a wave of conviction and godly sorrow.

Dear reader, if you have stuck with me to this point in my journey, you are to me an exquisite jewel in my treasure box. For I know that this is the inevitable point where people tend to form one of three opinions about me.

Team 1: "I can't believe she has gone through all this and continues to publicly teach the Bible. She may be redeemed, but I don't want to hear from someone who has chosen a path of so much disobedience and rebellion."

Team 2: "I can't believe she didn't share more of her story. I need more details if I'm going to trust who she says she is now. What kind of an affair was it? Did it cross the line—you know, *the* line? How can I be sure she is truly repentant? How can I be sure she's not a phony if I don't have specifics?"

Team 3: "Well, if this big of a screwup can be set free, then I certainly can be too!"

I want you to know here that I take full responsibility for what I did. I was completely entangled in a stronghold of sin, and this time I was very much the offender, not the victim. I betrayed, I lied, and I was a complete hypocrite to everyone I held dear.

The Light of Day

That day in March, at 12:30 p.m., when my secret sin hit the light of day, will forever be sealed in my memory as the worst and most beautiful day of my life.

I can barely write of it now without bursting into sobs. On one hand, it was as if I were waking up from a paralyzing coma, gasping for breath as all my senses were finally firing at full capacity again. At the same time, I was struck with a sense of impending doom. My mind was racing: *What will people say? Will my church disown me? Will Justin leave me? Will my children be forever tainted? Will my friends speak to me again?*

"Oh, Lord," I cried, "are you still there? Is it too late for my dream? Is it too late for *me*? Oh please, Lord, let it not be too late."

In the midst of my brokenness and these overpowering emotions, I saw a beautiful, life-altering vision of the love, mercy, and forgiveness that Jesus Christ had lavished upon me. This vision came and stood in front of me . . . in the form of my husband.

He had already forgiven me so much. I simply couldn't believe he would be able to extend grace and love to me once again—nor did I expect him to. And yet he did. If you ask him now, he will tell you that on that day he felt like his body was taken captive by a supernatural force—as if God's unseen hands were moving his words and thoughts as he listened to me and reacted to me.

Within moments after I'd replayed the nauseating events of the past three years to Justin—events that now tasted like sulfur in my mouth, burning my tongue—this man the Lord gave me to protect me, honor me, and love me as Christ loves his church made the impossible choice to love and forgive me despite his pain.

God's love and my husband's love should have been enough to carry me through the days of cleaning up the crash site that followed. However, as the vines of gossip and rumor began to spread their suffocating grasp through my small town, the arrows of condemning glances, unreturned phone calls, and rolled eyes pierced my skin with such torturous poison that I could barely breathe.

In a moment of sheer agony and selfishness, I chased a leftover bottle of Xanax with an aged bottle of wine and prayed for the Lord to end my life. That afternoon is forever burned into my memory: sitting alone on the cold, concrete floor, too numb to cry, with every bit of emotion in me dried up. I was overwhelmed with feelings of such worthlessness that I was sure my husband, children, and friends would just be better off without me. I just wanted it all to end. Had it not been for the intervention of one of my most dear and beloved friends, that might have been what happened.

I survived physically, but how does one come back to life emotionally and spiritually from a pit this deep? Stay with me, friend, and I will give you a glimpse into this humbling journey back to life.

I call the summer that followed my summer of sanctification. With the love and support of my husband and a handful of people who stood beside me, I spent the summer as a recluse in my home. For the first time in my life, I wanted nothing to do with the outside world—or at least not my hometown. I briefly attempted to reenter my normal ministry routine at church, but most people seemed shocked or, at the very least, put off by my attempt to serve. It was as if I had suddenly developed a bright red stamp on my forehead that read *sinner*. With all the gossip and rejection I experienced by people who used to be my friends, even a brief trip to Walmart would leave me in sobs and with a neck broken out in hives.

I just wanted to heal and find God again (who, by the way, had never moved). All summer long it took every ounce of energy to climb out of bed, and I am convinced that I had this amount of strength only because I'd made it my habit to recite the following psalm to the Lord each morning—mostly because I didn't know what else to say to him:

Have mercy on me, O God,
because of your unfailing love.
Because of your great compassion,
blot out the stain of my sins.
Wash me clean from my guilt.
Purify me from my sin.
For I recognize my rebellion;
it haunts me day and night.
Against you, and you alone, have I sinned;
I have done what is evil in your sight.
You will be proved right in what you say,
and your judgment against me is just.
For I was born a sinner—
yes, from the moment my mother conceived me.
But you desire honesty from the womb,
teaching me wisdom even there.

Purify me from my sins, and I will be clean;
  wash me, and I will be whiter than snow.
Oh, give me back my joy again;
  you have broken me—
  now let me rejoice.
Don't keep looking at my sins.
  Remove the stain of my guilt.
Create in me a clean heart, O God.
  Renew a loyal spirit within me.
Do not banish me from your presence,
  and don't take your Holy Spirit from me.

Restore to me the joy of your salvation,
  and make me willing to obey you.
Then I will teach your ways to rebels,
  and they will return to you.
Forgive me for shedding blood, O God who saves;
  then I will joyfully sing of your forgiveness.
Unseal my lips, O Lord,
  that my mouth may praise you.

You do not desire a sacrifice, or I would offer one.
  You do not want a burnt offering.
The sacrifice you desire is a broken spirit.
  You will not reject a broken and repentant heart, O God.
Look with favor on Zion and help her;
  rebuild the walls of Jerusalem.
Then you will be pleased with sacrifices offered in the right spirit—
  with burnt offerings and whole burnt offerings.
  Then bulls will again be sacrificed on your altar.

PSALM 51

I had to make a choice each morning to wake up and take one step closer to him. I had no idea how far I'd gone—three miles or three hundred—and each step back felt agonizing and exhausting. But I simply had to get back to him. For the first time in my life, he was my only hope. I had gotten so low that if the Lord was not as big as I was counting on him to be, I was most assuredly a dead woman. The only hope I had left to cling to was the hope David hung on to: "David also spoke of this when he described the happiness of those who are declared righteous without working for it: 'Oh, what joy for those whose disobedience is forgiven, whose sins are put out of sight. Yes, what joy for those whose record the LORD has cleared of sin'" (Romans 4:6-8).

Paul is quoting here from the psalm David wrote after confessing his affair with Bathsheba. In this passage David makes two beautiful statements that should thrill every one of us, regardless of our particular sin. First, God forgives our sin and grants us righteousness despite our works. Second, once we are forgiven, our sin is cleared from the heavenly record and is never counted against us. Wow! My eyes well up with tears at the mere thought of it. I am in humble agreement with David on this one: "Oh, what joy"!

The Lost Has Been Found

I know I'm not alone in having been far from God and needing to return to him. The story of the Prodigal Son, found in Luke 15:11-32, is a tragic and beautiful story of the sinfulness of a son and the goodness of a father. In a few short verses, Christ paints a brilliant picture of rebellion, repentance, return, and rejoicing.

As you read this passage, you will recognize this theme: the false promise of freedom that comes alongside sin only ends in slavery. The boy in this story thinks the grass is greener on the other side. He wants to make his own way, his own plans—far from the watchful eye of his father.

Once the share of his father's wealth is in hand, the young man travels to a distant land to party (or as the Bible puts it, to engage in "wild living"). As the young man soon discovers, however, we are always destined for trouble when we value the things money can buy more than the things money cannot buy.

No matter how long you've been away, it's never too late to let the goodness and love of your Lord finally overtake you.

Life in the distant country is not at all what the young man expected. Once the money runs out, his friends abandon him, and a famine sweeps through the land. The son is forced to do what he would not do for his father—work! Instead of getting a taste of freedom and relishing the finer things in life, he finds himself begging a local farmer to let him feed his pigs, just so he can eat the scraps he gives to the swine.

Can you imagine being there—penniless, starving, filthy, and so desperate that you wish you could eat the scraps you're dumping out of your bucket into the pen of pigs? I can relate all too well. I have been there—pigs included!

It's no surprise this young fellow finally says to himself, *What am I doing?* This is the first step toward repentance. To repent literally means to turn away or to change one's mind. And that is exactly what the young man does right there in the midst of the pigpen. He changes his mind about being dirty. He is finally ready for a good bath.

In verse 17 we read that the father's servants had more to eat at home than the young son did in this faraway land. On a personal level, this is an awesome reminder to us of two things: first, our Father, just like the boy's father, is still sitting at home. He has never moved away. He has never turned his back on us. He has always remained steady and firm. We are the ones who have a tendency to run. It is also interesting to note that it's the thought of the father's goodness that eventually causes the boy to wake up and head back home.

No matter how long you've been away, it's never too late to let the goodness and love of your Lord finally overtake you. Remember how much happier you were feasting with your Father than feeding on filth.

> While he was still a long way off, his father saw him and was filled with compassion for him; he ran to his son, threw his arms around him and kissed him.
>
> The son said to him, "Father, I have sinned against heaven and against you. I am no longer worthy to be called your son."
>
> But the father said to his servants, "Quick! Bring the best robe and put it on him. Put a ring on his finger and sandals on his feet. Bring the fattened calf and kill it. Let's have a feast and celebrate. For this son of mine was dead and is alive again; he was lost and is found." So they began to celebrate. LUKE 15:20-24 (NIV)

Do you know what I picture when the Scripture tells us that the boy is still a "long way off"? I picture an old Jewish man sitting on his porch in his rocker, watching the horizon. I imagine this man made a habit of coming out of his house each day as the sun was setting and just sitting, praying, and watching. You see, the prodigal doesn't even make it to the front yard before his father lays eyes on him.

I envision this old man squinting as he sees a faint object in the distance, his eyes growing wider as the object makes its way into clear view. And then, the most beautiful picture of all, this hopeful father musters every ounce of strength in his aging body as he leaps from his rocker and breaks into a full sprint toward the approaching object. Paying no attention to his aching knees and back, he needs no one to verify who is making his way to the house. He can recognize his own son simply by the shadow his body casts onto the ground. Can you see him? It is his son! His own flesh and blood! The one he has spent every day waiting for since his departure.

Before the son can even finish his apology in verse 21, the father is calling for the party to begin. If this isn't a picture of what it looks like to "forgive and forget," I don't know what is. Oh, how I pray you get this, dear one! This is a picture of what it looks like to our heavenly Father when you turn from your sin, repent, and come home to him. God is not standing at the door ready to point his condemning finger at you, nor has he moved on to other, more important matters needing his attention. No! He is there, waiting . . . watching . . . rejoicing.

The Father is rich in mercy and eager to forgive. He is anxious to embrace you. Why? For no other reason than that you are his child. Allow that truth to penetrate your being for a moment, and I'll get a tissue to wipe the tears from my keyboard while you ponder.

From Death to Life

Oh, how I pray that you are ending this chapter as a victor in Christ. It would absolutely thrill my heart to know your personal story. What a privilege it would be to dance at your celebration party! As we continue on in this journey together, please take hold of the fact that God desperately desires for you to be one who overcomes.

If you have spent any time in the younger brother's shoes, the thought that God is still for you, still longs for you, still desires you, and continues to unfold his beautiful tapestry of blessings in your life may seem unimaginable. Through my summer of sanctification I felt there was no one, not even my husband, who completely understood the inner workings of what I'd done, why I'd done it, and who I had become. There were also plenty of people who wanted to continually remind me of the filth of my sin. But, loved one, there is one who can see who you truly are and who you are capable of becoming. He sees into the recesses of your heart—past the hurt, past the abuse, past the anger, past the sorrow, past the sin—deep into a place where no human has ever had, nor will ever have, the power to enter.

> Take comfort in knowing God has your name on his lips as he kisses your brow and wipes the tears from your bloodshot eyes.

I pray that as you have studied about the Father's love and traveled this homecoming journey with me, you have taken this opportunity not just to walk but to *run* home into the captivating embrace of your heavenly Father. Once you are there, take a deep breath. And as you do, rest in his secure and loving arms. Let him hold you tightly; allow his heartbeat to pound against your tear-stained cheeks as you cling firmly to him. Do not be afraid.

Take comfort in knowing he has your name on his lips as he kisses your brow and wipes the tears from your bloodshot eyes. It is the name that he alone gave you—the name he whispered as he shaped and breathed life into your small, unformed body. It is the name not even the angels comprehend and you yourself will not know until he calls for you in glory. Until that time, however, it is the name otherwise known as . . . *child.* When Jesus gives a message to the churches about his future Kingdom, he offers these words of encouragement: "I will give to each one a white stone, and on the stone will be engraved a new name that no one understands except the one who receives it" (Revelation 2:17).

YOU ARE NAMED BY GOD: *You are his child.*

CHAPTER 10

Living under His Protection

THERE'S NO NEWS MORE WONDERFUL than knowing God has made you and named you his child! That means that, no matter where you go, you are under his care and his protection. But being his child also comes with a sobering warning: once you're God's child, you have also become a prime target.

As we go forward, let me be clear about this. From the moment you were extended the Holy Spirit on behalf of Jesus Christ, you were sealed—guaranteeing that you belong to him (see Ephesians 1:13, NIV). That imagery of being sealed brings to mind the mental picture of my grandmother using all the might in her aging hands to tightly screw the lid onto her homemade preserves. Once those peaches were sealed in the jar, there was no way any air could seep in to ruin them. And so it is with us—once we are sealed for God's purposes, no one can snatch us away—nor can we lose our position in eternity.

But even though Satan doesn't have the power to claim God's children for eternity, we still need to be on our guard against his evil schemes. He has one primary objective, and that is to hold us in a place of captivity to get us to do his will. That means we can't be ignorant about what Satan is up to.

Now please take this truth to heart: if you are a genuine Christ follower, Satan cannot get inside you—he cannot make you do anything. He can only manipulate circumstances to deceive you, to trick you into doing his will. And deceit is his specialty. He knows the human condition well, and he is well aware that we are quick to act on what we feel instead of on what we know.

In order to fend off assaults from our adversary, we must know who we're up against. Here are some of the descriptions Scripture gives us about Satan:

- Satan is continually looking for his next victim. He roams this earth, never sleeping, constantly prowling for easy prey (see Job 1:7).
- Satan is ferocious. Like roaring lions, he and his demons are on a hunt for blood (see 1 Peter 5:8).
- Satan not only desires for you to stumble and fall, but he desires for you to fall so hard that you turn your back on God (see Luke 22:3-4).
- Satan desires your life—not only in a spiritual sense, but in a physical sense as well (see Luke 13:16).

Satan's Prime Targets

If we were to imagine the type of person Satan would set his sights on, most of us would probably assume he'd take aim at the rebelling sinner. This woman has been told about Christ a dozen times, but she simply refuses to acknowledge him and seems to have no inclination toward faith at all. That guy has a reputation for getting drunk, swearing, and sleeping with a different woman every night. Surely *he* would be Satan's prime target.

Or what about the Christian slacker? Surely Satan would have his arrow pointed straight at her! I mean, she professes to be a Christian and she even goes to church on Sundays, but she "lives like hell" Monday through Saturday. She gossips at work, lies to her friends and coworkers, and has even been caught in multiple affairs. Yep, I'm sure *she* would be one of Satan's most sought-after targets!

Oh, but not *him*—he's our Bible study leader! He knows so much about the Bible. He really seems to have it all together. He's got a great job; people around town respect him; and he has a beautiful wife and kids. In fact, when the pastor's out of town, this guy fills in for him. No, Satan would be smart to keep away from this guy. He knows his stuff when it comes to God. He would never fall for some measly attack from Satan.

Please note: no one is exempt from Satan's schemes. He is the deceiver of *all* humankind, believer and unbeliever alike. He would love nothing more than for all flesh to perish so that no tongue could utter a word of praise to God again. Remember, Satan's real problem is not with humanity; his battle is with God. Satan (aka Lucifer) wanted the throne, the glory, the worship, but God Almighty said, "I don't think so . . ." (see Isaiah 14:12-15).

So Satan is mad at God. He is angry and bitter and loathes the fact that God is all-powerful. And because Satan is too weak to make a direct hit on the Almighty himself, who do you think is his next target? You got it. The *child* of the Almighty. The passionate pursuer of Christ.

He knows how frail we are. But he has also given us what we need to fight back against our enemy.

Did you catch that? Satan's prime target is not the rebelling sinner or the Christian slacker. It's the sincerely devoted follower of Christ. In fact, the more powerful your story, the more captivating your love, the more fervent your passion—the more watchful the murderous eye of Satan will be on you.

When a righteous one falls, fellow believers often gasp in disbelief. Some think, *Well, I didn't see that one coming. She seemed to have it all together!* or *I can't believe he did that. He must not have been a true Christian after all,* or *I can't believe I used to think so highly of her. I should have seen right through her charade.*

When a fellow Christian goes from walking upright to lying face down in the mud, brothers and sisters in Christ tend to stand back in shock and judgment. But understand one thing: our God is not taken off guard. He knows how frail we are. But he has also given us what we need to fight back against our enemy.

I pray that, as you read this chapter, a new sense of urgency overtakes you. I pray that you will become more aware of Satan's desire to devour and destroy you so you can be ready when you become his next target.

Have you been seduced in your past? Are you being seduced in your present? Since we are all targets at some point in our lives, it is essential that we be able to spot the warning signs so we can recognize when we're under attack.

Warning #1: An attack is common following a period of spiritual rejuvenation

As Jesus' ministry goes public, big things start happening. Talk about spiritual high points—here he gets baptized, sees heaven opening, has the Spirit of God come upon him, and hears the very voice of God speaking out of heaven!

> As soon as Jesus was baptized, he went up out of the water.
> At that moment heaven was opened, and he saw the Spirit of
> God descending like a dove and alighting on him. And a voice
> from heaven said, "This is my Son, whom I love; with him
> I am well pleased."
> Then Jesus was led by the Spirit into the wilderness to be
> tempted by the devil. MATTHEW 3:16–4:1 (NIV)

I can't imagine a more direct encounter of blessing! But then, almost immediately, Christ undergoes a direct attack from Satan—he is led into the desert to be tempted. Jesus' example shows us that we don't necessarily have to be participating in ungodly activities for seduction to hit. Satan loves nothing more than to put out the flame of a burning believer, someone who is on fire for the Lord.

Peter is another example of someone who is tempted right on the heels of spiritual success. Peter is one of the most passionate pursuers of Christ in all of Scripture, yet Satan knows his weak points, and he does all he can to cause Peter's roaring flame to dwindle into nothing more than smoldering coals.

Not only is Peter one of the first to leave everything and follow Jesus, but he also has had a number of mountaintop experiences with his Lord. He is an eyewitness to the healing of his mother-in-law (see Matthew 8:14-15), he is the only disciple with the courage to get out of the boat and walk on the water to Jesus (see Matthew 14:22-33), and he is one of three allowed to stand in Jesus' presence as he is transformed into glorious brilliance (see Matthew 17:1-13). Peter even makes a public declaration that, even if everyone else abandons Jesus, he will stand by him no matter what (see Matthew 26:33).

And yet on the heels of these peak spiritual experiences, Peter is tempted to turn his back on his Savior at the very darkest moment of Jesus' life. Peter, a man who keeps close company with the God made flesh and loves him passionately, denies that he even knows him (see Matthew 26:74).

When you come down from the mountaintop, be on your guard. Don't think you're immune from Satan's poison just because you're coming off a spiritual encounter. In fact, that's the time Satan wants you most.

Warning #2: An attack of Satan is shrouded in secrecy

Secrets are not always evil in nature, but evil almost always starts out in secret. And when a secret is whispered into your ear from the lying tongue of the serpent, you can be sure there is evil oozing all over it. The Bible puts it this way: "This lawlessness is already at work secretly, and it will remain secret until the one who is holding it back steps out of the way" (2 Thessalonians 2:7).

Secrecy is one of Satan's most powerful strongholds.

I am two years older than my brother. When we were children, I tended to use my age against him. I would force him to play girly games with me, like Barbie and dress-up. There were times when he would refuse to play and I in turn reacted out of sheer meanness. I would say hurtful words to him to try to guilt him into playing my game of choice. Sometimes my words hurt him so much that he would run straight to our mother and, with tears streaming down his cheeks, repeat the "mean sister" words to her.

My mother would inevitably confront me: "Kasey, did you say this to your brother?" And what do you think my response was? That's right—a bald-faced lie! In order to save my bottom from a blisterin', I would say anything to cover my wrong. The thing is, though, even if I escaped punishment from my mom, my lies never succeeded in clearing my conscience.

Our enemy, who is known as the "father of lies" (John 8:44), finds great pleasure in using our secrets against us. He wants us to fear the discipline of our Father and the correction of the godly people around us so much that we spend all our energy covering up our dark, hidden places. Secrecy is one of Satan's most powerful strongholds. I encourage you to take a moment to examine your words and actions. Do they hold up in the light of day? If not, they ought to have no place in your life. In other words, if you are saying or doing something that could not be posted on a giant billboard for the entire town to see and be proud of, you should not be saying or doing it at all.

Warning #3: An attack of Satan leaves you feeling powerless
Scripture leaves no doubt about the impact sin can have on us. Isaiah 64:6 puts it this way: "We are all infected and impure with sin. When we display our righteous deeds, they are nothing but filthy rags. Like autumn leaves, we wither and fall, and our sins sweep us away like the wind."

The visual from this verse is so powerful for me. Picture a shriveled leaf falling from a tree and being whisked away by the breeze. It tosses and turns in its flight, eventually crashing to the cold, hard ground. Receiving a blow from Satan has similar results. Many people who find themselves in a habitual pattern of sin don't seem to recognize how far they're being blown off course. Like that leaf being tossed around by the breeze, they feel utterly powerless to stop their destructive behavior.

The book of Hebrews describes sin in equally sobering terms: "Let us throw off everything that hinders and the sin that so easily entangles. And let us run with perseverance the race marked out for us" (12:1, NIV).

Now picture a spiderweb, intricately crafted with the greatest of detail. As you marvel at the sight of how something so small could create something so ornate, you watch a tiny bug fly smack-dab into the middle of the masterpiece. You look on as the bug wiggles and flutters with all its might. It makes every attempt to break free from the sticky web, but to no avail. Little does the bug know this web was designed specifically to trap it!

And so it is with Satan. His ammo is tailor made for each of us, specially crafted to trip us up. Child of God, the enemy doesn't usually present us with big, obvious sins right away. Instead, he takes something that seems small and fairly harmless, and then wraps it up with shiny paper and puts a big bow on top. Satan's plan of attack begins with tiny pieces of deception, but his ultimate goal is total captivity!

Let's go back to our friend Peter (also called Simon) for a moment. Just before Jesus' death, Jesus gives some final instructions to his disciples, along with this warning: "Simon, Simon,

Satan has asked to sift each of you like wheat" (Luke 22:31). *Sift* in this passage literally means "to separate and scatter"—to drive away from God and the good plans he has for his followers. That is exactly what Satan desires to do to us, too. He wants to separate us from the will of God and scatter us around until we are a big, destructive mess!

The point of walking through these warning signs together is not to scare you but to wake you up. Satan's seduction is serious business. He has only one end result in mind: total destruction.

Take a moment to look at your present and evaluate the warning signs you see. What areas of doubt, fear, shame, bitterness, envy, or blame are seeping in, gradually making their way into your speech, thoughts, actions, and relationship with God? Maybe the lie is ever so subtle at this point. It's as if the beautifully spun spiderweb is still in the distance, but it's getting closer and closer in your line of vision as you fly toward it. Or maybe you have just been caught in the web and are fighting frantically to break free. Or maybe, just maybe, you have been stuck in the web for some time now. You are tired, out of breath, and sore from trying to fight your way out. As your vision fades, you experience a sense of powerlessness like you've never felt before.

> Even when we are tempted to give up and have lost all hope, the Lord remains faithful.

Whatever the case, don't give up! The day of evil is here, and the battle lines have been drawn. It's time for us to stand our ground. No matter how weak we feel, we can be confident that Christ is stronger than our enemy. "He has rescued us from the kingdom of darkness and transferred us into the Kingdom of his dear Son, who purchased our freedom and forgave our sins" (Colossians 1:13-14). If you are a child of God, you have been rescued and redeemed from sin and judgment!

Even when we feel most powerless, we can take comfort in the Lord's promise that he will strengthen us to fight. "The Lord is faithful; he will strengthen you and guard you from the evil one" (2 Thessalonians 3:3). What an amazing truth! I pray you will take a moment to bask in that verse. Even when we are tempted to give up and have lost all hope, the Lord remains faithful. We can rest securely in the mighty arms of our faithful protector.

YOU ARE NAMED BY GOD: *You are safe.*

CHAPTER 11

Broken but Beautiful

*No one who is born of God will continue to sin, because
God's seed remains in them; they cannot go on sinning,
because they have been born of God.* 1 JOHN 3:9 (NIV)

WHEN I FIRST READ this passage of Scripture, I was terrified. At
the time I was a mom of two children under the age of five, which
meant I had to try to squeeze in my quiet times during those rare
moments when there wasn't a kid in need of something. I would
leave my Bible open on the kitchen table throughout the day—
partly because its simple presence in the center of our household
seemed to comfort me, but mostly to remind me to snatch a few
moments with it whenever I could.

I don't recall exactly how I ended up in 1 John, but on that
particular day—a sunny spring afternoon, fresh off my birthday—
that's where I found myself during my kitchen-table devotions.
I remember sitting at the table, frozen on this verse as a wave of
doubt and terror overcame me. Suddenly I started questioning
everything I'd believed all these years. Was I really going to heaven?

How did I know I was really a Christian? I mean, surely a *real* Christian wouldn't be struggling with sin as much as I was.

My personal sin at this point wasn't something you might categorize as a "big sin." But it was a sin all the same, and it was a sin I utterly hated. The worst part was that it was becoming more and more habitual and debilitating with each day that passed. I knew it was wrong. I knew I was hurting myself and others by allowing it to be part of my life. And I knew God desired more *from* me and more *for* me.

As humans, we tend to look at our behavior in terms of a sin scale. For example, murder=really bad; worry=not so bad. It's true that the murderer and the worrier may face different consequences and discipline as a result of their sin, but the Lord is much more interested in a person's heart. God sees each one of us, the sinner and the saint, in need of his grace and mercy, with no priority given to the category of sin. The Lord tells Samuel that he has different scales than we have as humans: "The LORD doesn't see things the way you see them. People judge by outward appearance, but the LORD looks at the heart" (1 Samuel 16:7).

As I sat at the kitchen table that day, I knew two things for certain: I didn't want to be consumed by any sin—large or small. I also knew that I loved Jesus Christ desperately. That fact alone snapped me back to the truth. In a strange way, that sense of conviction over my sin was a relief, because it showed that God wasn't finished with me. This kind of sorrow, after all, is evidence that you are the real deal. Being a Christian doesn't mean you will never again be tempted to sin. But it does mean you will experience a significant amount of guilt and disgust over your choice to sin. Not only that, but in the midst of your self-disgust, you will also find yourself craving the comfort and love of your heavenly Father like never before. And that, my friend, is one way to know you are the genuine artifact!

The Good Kind of Sorrow

Just a few days after I read 1 John 3:9, God led me to this other Scripture: "Godly sorrow brings repentance that leads to salvation and leaves no regret, but worldly sorrow brings death" (2 Corinthians 7:10, NIV).

There's the answer—the word that stings your heart. *Sorrow.*

And we're not talking about just any sorrow, but *godly* sorrow. Some people understand this as your conscience—that little voice in your head that tells you right from wrong. Christ followers know it as the Holy Spirit. Before Jesus ascended to heaven, he gave this encouragement to his followers about the Holy Spirit (also called the Advocate): "It is best for you that I go away, because if I don't, the Advocate won't come. If I do go away, then I will send him to you. And when he comes, he will convict the world of its sin, and of God's righteousness, and of the coming judgment" (John 16:7-8).

> If you are longing for ultimate restoration of your present, you must let God break your heart for whatever sin is holding you back from his complete control over your life.

We've established that it is not a matter of *if* we will sin, but *when.* We all sin, believers and unbelievers alike. The difference is that unbelievers sin with no remorse. The book of Isaiah puts it this way: "The look on their faces testifies against them; they parade their sin like Sodom; they do not hide it" (3:9, NIV).

Unbelievers go about their day with no guilt over their gossip, hatred, and betrayal. Believers, on the other hand, have the same capacity to sin, but suffering and guilt await them on the other side. That pain in your gut that keeps you up at night? Yep, that's it—the godly sorrow of conviction.

The Holy Spirit is always ready to warn us of the red flags of sin that lie ahead. However, it is our responsibility to invite him to fill us—and then listen when he speaks to us. Romans 8:26 tells us that the Holy Spirit "helps us in our weakness" if we are faithfully surrendered to him.

So what is conviction, really? Conviction is when a person is made conscious of his or her guilt (see Psalm 38:1-22). When that sting of conviction hits you, it doesn't always result in immediate sorrow, nor does it necessarily result in instant repentance. In biblical terms, repentance means to be sorry, to change one's mind, to turn back to God (see 2 Corinthians 7:10). Our flesh can become so resistant to the feeling of sorrow toward our sin that at times conviction only feels like a faint prick on our hearts. But whether it's a faint prick, a moderate sting, or a forceful stab, if you are a genuine follower of Christ the feeling will continue to produce pain in your life. It will ache and throb, refusing to leave you alone until you finally take your sin to the Lord.

If you are longing for ultimate restoration of your present, you must let God break your heart for whatever sin is holding you back from his complete control over your life. You must be willing to do the terrifying task of asking the Lord to consume you with godly sorrow. And it may be helpful to note here that this kind of sorrow usually starts with a choice, not a feeling.

Throughout my season of sin, I found myself coming before the Lord almost daily to ask his forgiveness. But it wasn't until godly sorrow came over me that true repentance was ushered in. You see, my Lord was faithful to forgive me each and every time I came to him, but his forgiveness alone did not break the habit of sin in my life (see David's story in 2 Samuel 12). To break the habit, I had to be broken myself. Only then could I begin to work toward the healing and restoration I needed and desired. Being sorry wasn't enough; I needed to be *sorrowful*—and ready to change.

As I look back now, I regret that it took me so long to come to a point of conviction and godly sorrow. Why did I give sin a foothold instead of squelching it immediately? I believe there are three main reasons why we allow ourselves to be seduced by Satan instead of being broken by God.

1. Fear of the Consequences

One of the big reasons we hold back from confessing our sin to God is that we fear divine consequences. It's true that consequences for our sin will inevitably come, but it's not because God desires more pain or grief for us (we bring that on ourselves). To the contrary, God uses consequences and discipline to bring us back on track with him, as well as to serve as tools of healing and restoration.

As scary as the unknown consequences may seem, we must trust our heavenly Father's heart—that he rejoices over our return to him and that he wants to bring us full freedom from the bondage of sin. However, he will do this in his own way, through the consequences he knows are best.

And let's be honest—were you getting anywhere doing it your way?

Take Jonah, for instance. He attempted to do things his own way, and the only place it got him is in the gut of a fish! Many people view Jonah as a children's story or a made-up allegory. However, Scripture is clear that Jonah was a real person . . . with real problems (see 2 Kings 14:25).

We are introduced to Jonah in the book that bears his name. He is a Jewish prophet in the northern kingdom of Israel from 793 to 753 BC. On one memorable occasion, God instructs him to carry a special message on his behalf to the other side of the train tracks, if you know what I mean—to one of Israel's biggest enemies: Assyria.

This call seems a little too crazy, even for a prophet like Jonah. In his incredulous state, Jonah forgets what an honor it is to hear God's Word and have the opportunity to obey. And when his fear gets the best of him, Jonah hitches a ride on a boat heading the complete opposite direction of the Lord's voice. As a note of application here, whenever the word of the Lord comes to us, disobedience is never the best option—no matter how crazy the call may be.

Long story short, Jonah disobeys and flees in the opposite direction of God's will. He ends up on a boat full of pagan idol worshipers who eventually throw him overboard. Although Jonah seems destined to drown, he winds up in the belly of a great fish (we like to call it a whale in Sunday school lessons, but who really knows) for three days and three nights.

As outlandish as this may seem to us, God actually uses this time to heal and restore Jonah. In fact, it is God who has Jonah thrown overboard and God who sends the fish to swallow him!

Finally, after three days, Jonah prays to the Lord from inside the fish. He says, "I cried out to the LORD in my great trouble, and he answered me. I called to you from the land of the dead, and LORD, you heard me! You threw me into the ocean depths, and I sank down to the heart of the sea" (Jonah 2:1-3).

When the fish spits Jonah onto dry land, God gives Jonah a do-over. (And praise the Lord for do-overs!) Yes, the consequences for Jonah are tough, but they enable Jonah to do the will of God, which he eventually does.

The moral of the Jonah story, however, is not that Jonah gets back up after being disciplined by God. It's the fact that God allows Jonah to get back up after his disobedience. And he will allow you to get back up too—you can count on it!

2. Fear of What People Might Think or Say

The second reason people shy away from brokenness before God is the fear of other people's reactions. If you focus on what people will say, it will hinder everything good you try to do. (I should know—this was the main reason behind my own extended stay in the pit.) I had been a witness to God's beautiful redemption many times in my past. I knew firsthand that he is mighty to save. It was the *people* in my life I was more afraid of.

> Trust a former pleaser on this—you do not want to pay the price of pleasing people rather than pleasing God.

Why do we care so much about what other people think? Why do we allow their comments to plague our thoughts, to push us to the brink of tears, to keep us in bed all day with the covers pulled over our faces? People pleasers, pay attention! For many women, the thought of having another woman not like us is almost more

unbearable than the pains of childbirth! I've been there myself—
I would rather be eight centimeters dilated with no epidural than
go through the pain of feeling unloved.

To receive ultimate healing from our sin, we must make a pact
between us and God. We must give over to him every worry about
what people will say or think about us, as well as every desire to
defend ourselves to those people. It is God's responsibility, not
ours, to bring the talk of others in check. And as we grow into
new, more Christlike versions of ourselves, humbled and broken
by our sin, the gossips will begin to find their lunch break much
more uneventful!

In Exodus 32 we see a vivid example of what happens when a
beloved child of God chooses to give in to the pressures of people
instead of the calling of the Lord. Aaron is the right-hand man
of his brother, Moses, during their confrontations with Pharaoh
and the Israelites' eventual escape from slavery in Egypt. Although
Aaron is a trusted leader and priest in the Israelite camp, he seems
to struggle with that timeless problem of people pleasing. Moses
(the Israelites' leader) has been atop a mountain, meeting with the
Lord for forty days and forty nights, and Aaron has been left in
charge in his absence. Although God's chosen people have promised to stay faithful to the Lord, they start getting impatient for
Moses' return, and grumbling begins to spread through the camp
like wildfire.

I picture Aaron doing his best to be patient along with everyone
else, but eventually he starts getting worn down under the pressure
of so many complaining voices. Eventually it takes just one whiner
yammering outside Aaron's tent: "Where is Moses? Where is God?
Did they abandon us?" Finally Aaron caves under the pressure

of the people's complaints, and all hell (literally) breaks loose in the camp. Before you know it, Israel's lust for idols makes them hungry for sin, and Aaron feeds their appetites by giving them just what they are whining for.

> All the people took the gold rings from their ears and brought them to Aaron. Then Aaron took the gold, melted it down, and molded it into the shape of a calf. When the people saw it, they exclaimed, "O Israel, these are the gods who brought you out of the land of Egypt!"
>
> Aaron saw how excited the people were, so he built an altar in front of the calf. Then he announced, "Tomorrow will be a festival to the LORD!"
>
> The people got up early the next morning to sacrifice burnt offerings and peace offerings. After this, they celebrated with feasting and drinking, and they indulged in pagan revelry. EXODUS 32:3-6

The fear of what people would say deafens Aaron to the voice of God. And the consequences are severe: the death of three thousand men by the sword, a plague in the camp, and worst of all, the temporary removal of the Lord's presence from the camp (see Exodus 32:27–33:3).

Listening to the voices of people over the voice of the Lord will always be costly. Trust a former pleaser on this—you do not want to pay the price of pleasing people rather than pleasing God. So move forward based on his voice alone, and do not cave to the opinions and attitudes of others. I assure you, it will not be to them that you give an account of your life.

3. Fear That God Will Not Be There to Catch You

The third main reason we tend to avoid revealing our sin to the light of day is that we believe Satan's lie that God won't be there to embrace us when we do. But God already proved himself faithful when he humbled himself on the cross and died for sins he did not commit. Not only do we have a God who is there to catch us when we fall, but we have a Savior who is the best defense attorney this world has to offer (even when we have a case that would never stand up in court). Christ is our advocate, pleading before God on our behalf. He does not want us to suffer for a crime he has already paid the penalty for (see 1 John 2:1). So we can put our hope solidly in the assurance that he will catch and defend us.

As frightening as it may seem to bring your sin before God, it is much more terrifying to be separated from him.

As Hebrews 10:23 says, we can "hold tightly without wavering to the hope we affirm, for God can be trusted to keep his promise."

In Luke 23 we see a beautiful picture of how God will not turn his back on sinners who cry out to him. The scene is at the cross—the one crucial moment that the entirety of the Bible leans toward. Jesus is crucified around 9:00 a.m., and he hangs on that cross for six excruciating hours, experiencing a kind of agony you and I will never fathom.

As our Lord remains nailed to the cross, a thief hangs on one side of him, vomiting out mockery and hatred. On the other side hangs another thief, yet there is something different about this man. Despite his past, this sinner chooses to believe that he, too, can be saved if this Jesus truly is God made flesh.

And right there, with mere moments of breath to spare, amid

his own pain and torment, the Lord grants the thief not only for-giveness but also a place with him in paradise (see Luke 23:42-43). Now that, my friend, is a God who is there to catch you.

. . .

As frightening as it may seem to bring your sin before God, it is much more terrifying to be separated from him. What I've learned since I first read 1 John 3:9 is that while there is an element of healthy fear to being a true child of God, when we are on the other side of repentance, we also find a beautiful promise. For when we are born of God, we receive a new name, a fresh start, and the gift of the Holy Spirit dwelling within us.

YOU ARE NAMED BY GOD: *You are free from the power of sin.*

CHAPTER 12

Believing God

FOR TWO YEARS MY HUSBAND AND I had been praying for God to move us—literally. We didn't know if it would be down the street or across the world, but we could both sense in our spirits that the Lord was beginning the process of uprooting us from all that was comfortable. At the time everything was going well—Justin had a secure job and a steady income, I was able to stay home with the children, we had a newly built two-story home, and we had an intimate group of friends nearby. Oh, and did I mention that I was the third generation from my family in our town? Everything was good—maybe too good. So Justin and I started doing what we tend to do when things seem too good to be true: we started praying.

Almost two years to the day from when we started praying, the Lord flung open the doors for us to move to another town.

It may not have been an obvious "God thing" to our family, friends, or community, but to Justin and me it was crystal clear. Not only was God opening tangible doors for us to move, but he also gave both of us an overwhelming sense of peace and provision about it. With every step forward we took, the Lord kept affirming this calling through a bombardment of excitement and joy within our spirits.

And so we packed up everything we owned, enrolled our daughter into her first year of public school, and rented a small home within a few blocks of the school. We had no friends or family there—not one connection except for the people in Justin's new office. We had no church, no specific sense of direction, no idea if the school we picked was a good one or if Emma Grace had been placed with a good teacher. We had practically no room to sit in our new rental (except on top of one another). We didn't know our neighbors, and we didn't even know how to get to Walmart. Suddenly we were responsible for a monthly mortgage *and* a rent payment. And, most startling of all, Justin had an exciting new job, but he was making less than half his previous salary.

Crazy, you say? Well, yes, it was. Most leaps of faith are.

But can I tell you one more vitally important piece of our leap? My family has never been happier.

· · ·

When God calls us to do something, he wants us to respond to his leading based on faith, not on what seems logical to other people or what we have seen him do in the past. As we walk with him into the unknown, he desires our complete trust—based on the fact that he is God and we are not!

When God calls people, he doesn't always choose those with the best résumés. His number one requirement is that they will believe him and follow him, even through the craziest and most inexplicable circumstances. Prime case study from the Old Testament: Abram (later known as Abraham).

If you have ever felt unworthy or unqualified to believe that God will fulfill great purposes in your life, please allow me to introduce you to Abram. What you may not know about him is that at the time of his dramatic call from the Lord, he is living in idolatry. Abram is not yet worshiping the one true God; he is following many "little *g*" gods along with the rest of his family (see Joshua 24:2). He does not know the Creator of the universe, who is about to unleash his power into his destiny. In short, when our story begins, Abram is an unbeliever.

> When God calls people, he doesn't always choose those with the best résumés.

Abram lives in the land of Ur, a trading mecca close to the Euphrates River devoted to the worship of Nannar, the moon god. At seventy-five years old, Abram is considered one of the most educated and successful members of his family. Although Abram and his wife, Sarai (also his half sister), are childless, they are likely pretty content in their flourishing civilization, surrounded by their closest friends and family. And then one day, out of nowhere, Abram experiences a revolutionary moment that changes not only the course of his life but the lives of all humankind as we know it.

The Lord had said to Abram, "Leave your native country, your relatives, and your father's family, and go to the land that

I will show you. I will make you into a great nation. I will bless you and make you famous, and you will be a blessing to others. I will bless those who bless you and curse those who treat you with contempt. All the families on earth will be blessed through you." GENESIS 12:1-3

When God calls Abram and his family to leave their contented life, Abram might be doing any number of things—working out in the fields, spending some time thinking on a mountaintop, sitting with his family around the supper table, or simply watching the passersby in the town square. What we do know is that when God calls Abram to leave his hometown and start walking, Abram obeys.

When the Word of God comes into Abram's life, all other gods fail in comparison to the one true God. In that moment a miracle of faith is born, and the stage is now set for the redemptive process that eventually threads its way through history. Abram is first in a line of people God calls as his chosen ones—regardless of who they are or what they have done—through their faith alone.

Abram's next move should be a wake-up call for all of us who desire more of God in our lives. Genesis 12:4 tells us simply, "So Abram went, as the LORD had told him" (NIV). The interesting part is that Abram has no idea where God is taking him. The only navigational information given by the Lord is that he will show Abram. But that is enough. Abram packs up everything and leaves his home, his friends, and some of his extended family to embark on this blind journey God has called him to. Abram believes God even though he doesn't know where, how, when, or why.

I doubt Abram realized at that moment how his decision to believe God would affect not just his personal history but the history of the entire world. It's after Abram agrees to follow wholeheartedly that the Lord makes a mighty promise to a childless old man: "The Lord took Abram outside and said to him, 'Look up into the sky and count the stars if you can. That's how many descendants you will have!' And Abram believed the Lord, and the Lord counted him as righteous because of his faith" (Genesis 15:5-6).

God not only calls Abram to greatness, but he also secures Abram through his stamp of approval on his life—otherwise known as his covenant. And God doesn't play around with covenants. They represent the promises he makes to his children—promises that ensure the Lord's great plan will be fulfilled in spite of our weaknesses, struggles, and sins.

A New Name

God chooses an interesting seal to signify his promise of making Abram into the father of many generations. He does it through a name change. God tells Abram, "This is my covenant with you: I will make you the father of a multitude of nations! What's more, I am changing your name. It will no longer be Abram. Instead, you will be called Abraham, for you will be the father of many nations" (Genesis 17:4-5).

Perhaps your given name has some special significance—maybe it was chosen in honor of a family member or your parents liked the meaning or it's just a crazy combination of your parents and the '70s. Kasey is my given name from my earthly parents, and outside of their just liking the name and wanting it to begin with a *K*, it held no special meaning for them. In Bible times, though, names weren't just chosen for the letter they started with or the way they rolled off the tongue. Names were significant in that they recorded where someone came from (his or her birth family), and they often communicated a message about the person's character or legacy. Abram, for example, means "exalted father."

When the Lord changes Abram's name to Abraham, his name now means "father of a multitude." This is a defining moment in the relationship between Abraham and the Lord. It is a reaffirmation of God's promise to Abraham to multiply his family. What a beautiful gift from God—that whenever someone calls to him from out in the field or whenever Sarah speaks to him across the dinner table, the very name *Abraham* is a personal reminder of the Lord's faithfulness and call on his life.

And so it is for any of us who have surrendered our old lives to new life in Jesus Christ. Like Abram, we have been given God's covenant promise that he will use us for his great purposes in spite of ourselves. Jesus himself is our seal and promise of that covenant. The Holy Spirit is God's guarantee that he is who he says he is and that he will do what he has promised. When we are "sealed" by the indwelling of the Spirit, we belong to Jesus Christ, and nothing and no one can take us from him. The Spirit within us is a down payment that we will one day receive glorified bodies and join Jesus in eternal glory (see 2 Corinthians 1:20-22, NIV).

Like Abram, we have been given a new identity. As we take on the character of Christ, we also have the privilege of taking on his name: *Christian*. The name was first given to the disciples in Syrian Antioch during the 40s of the first century (see Acts 11:26), and it means "of or belonging to Christ." That new name defines who I am and who I want to become.

The book of Revelation indicates that there's another name God has in mind for us—but this one is personalized, unique to each follower of Christ. And it hasn't been revealed yet. "All who are victorious will become pillars in the Temple of my God, and they will never have to leave it. And I will write on them the name of my God, and they will be citizens in the city of my God—the new Jerusalem that comes down from heaven from my God. And I will also write on them my new name" (Revelation 3:12). Sometimes I imagine the trumpet sounding when Christ returns and hearing a new name ringing in my ear from his mouth—a name that was formed in the depths of the darkness as he hovered over the formless earth. I imagine hearing this name for the first time and having every pore on my skin feel as though I am finally home.

Becoming an Abraham

One of the keys to a total transformation of our present is to do an honest evaluation of our belief system. There are many people all over the world who believe in God. There are plenty of good, moral people who worship in church services all over the country. But belief on its own is not enough to take a leap of faith the way Abraham did.

In order to be transformed, we must come to the realization that it is not enough to simply believe in God; we must believe *God*.

What type of a believer are you? Are you simply a good person, or is there a depth of Christian love inside you that others have difficulty comprehending? Do you boldly step out in faith, even when you are unable to understand the why or see the end result? Do you seek to know and follow him even when the stakes are high? How far are you willing to go to follow the Lord? Like Abraham, are you willing to let go of what you know, to leave the comforts of your world behind?

No more mundane! No more ordinary! No more stagnant Christianity! We need to be the Abrahams of our day!

In order to be transformed into that Abrahamic faith, we must come to the realization that it is not enough to simply believe *in* God; we must believe *God*. We must believe who he is and what he says, and trust that he will keep his promises in our lives.

The choice is up to you. You are the only one who can pick up your stuff, leave your friends and possessions and relatives behind, and go. And let me just remind you that you might be called to do all this with no idea about where you're going!

No Mistake

If there is one passage of Scripture that totally captivates me in my deepest moments of doubt, it is Psalm 139. These verses are a warm blanket over my coldest and most tender places.

> You created my inmost being;
> > you knit me together in my mother's womb.
> I praise you because I am fearfully and wonderfully made;
> > your works are wonderful,
> > I know that full well.
> My frame was not hidden from you
> > when I was made in the secret place,
> > when I was woven together in the depths of the earth.
> Your eyes saw my unformed body;
> > all the days ordained for me were written in your book
> > before one of them came to be. PSALM 139:13-16 (NIV)

Have you ever laid eyes on such beautiful words in all your life?

I have found myself repeating this portion of Scripture countless times in the darkness of my bedroom—at times when my eyes should have been peacefully shut but were glued open instead. Is it just me, or does it seem as if the dark brings out the worst in you? I can be doing fine in the light of day, but when night falls and I'm left to the quietness of my thoughts, it's as if Satan (who has apparently been hiding under the bed all day) begins to creep out from under the mattress and whisper directly into the weakest spots in my armor.

Maybe that's why I feel the need to repeat the words of that psalm over and over. Frankly, sometimes I find it hard to believe that my Creator pieced my body together, with the greatest of detail, inside the safety of my mother's womb. Just as a quilter carefully weaves in each thread, attaching the squares until a beautiful masterpiece has been completed, so your Father intricately pieced together your skin, your nose, your eyes, your mouth.

You are no mistake. Jesus did not bleed and die for a mistake.

Not only that, but he also chose how many days you would spend on this earth in this temporary dwelling. He ordained all your days, and even now, that secret number is listed in the Lord's personal journal.

At what moments do the greatest feelings of doubt strike you? Is it when you lie down at night? When you gaze into the mirror? When a certain friend or family member speaks to you in *that* tone? Is it when you're sitting in your office, questioning your purpose? When your spouse seems distant or your children don't respect your authority?

If you're ever plagued by doubt, know that you are not alone. Humans have been tempted ever since the very beginning.

The serpent was the shrewdest of all the wild animals the LORD God had made. One day he asked the woman, "Did God really say you must not eat the fruit from any of the trees in the garden?"

"Of course we may eat fruit from the trees in the garden," the woman replied. "It's only the fruit from the tree in the middle of the garden that we are not allowed to eat. God said, 'You must not eat it or even touch it; if you do, you will die.'"

"You won't die!" the serpent replied to the woman. "God knows that your eyes will be opened as soon as you eat it, and you will be like God, knowing both good and evil."

The woman was convinced. She saw that the tree was beautiful and its fruit looked delicious, and she wanted the wisdom it would give her. So she took some of the fruit and ate it. Then she gave some to her husband, who was with her, and he ate it, too. GENESIS 3:1-6

There's that cunning tempter again!

"You won't die!" Satan says to Eve. And there it is—the first seed of doubt in all of Scripture. Eve knows her God. She has walked with him and talked with him and was personally made by him. She also knew what God said: "You may freely eat the fruit of every tree in the garden—except the tree of the knowledge of good and evil. If you eat its fruit, you are sure to die" (Genesis 2:16-17).

There is no stuttering or stammering on the part of our Lord here—just a simple, straightforward instruction. God leaves no room for doubt or misinterpretation. In fact, he gives Adam and

Eve ample selections of fruit and veggies, plenty of produce to feast on for centuries to come. It's only this one tree that's off limits.

And don't think that Satan doesn't already know exactly what God said before he asks Eve the question. He also knows that it has to be Eve's idea to follow through with the sin. He can't pick the fruit himself and give it to her; he has to seduce her to make that decision all on her own. And how does he do that? You got it—by placing tiny crumbs of doubt on the ground for her to pick up. Unfortunately for Eve's sake and for the future of humanity, those seeds lead straight to the fall of all humankind.

Can you see the wheels of doubt turning in Eve's mind? *Maybe God made a mistake. Maybe he meant the tree on the other side of the Garden, not this one.* We don't know exactly what Eve's justifications were, but they were enough to make her doubt God's words and his character. Once the seeds of Satan-induced doubt take root, the branches begin to grow in our minds, affecting our thoughts, our speech, and ultimately our actions.

The book of James gives some insight about our human tendency toward doubt, especially as it relates to prayer: "You must believe and not doubt, because the one who doubts is like a wave of the sea, blown and tossed by the wind" (1:6, NIV). Have you ever stood on the beach and watched as the huge waves maintain their constant motion of restlessness? These waves are not only restless; they are driven by outside forces such as the wind and the tide. Doubt can do the same thing to you. It is driven by an outside force (Satan), and it can cause you to feel restless and unsettled.

In our moments of weakness, it is easy to allow Satan's lies to tempt us to doubt. And the biggest area Satan desires to cover with doubt is the core of who we are as believers in Christ—our meaning, our value, our self-worth. But Scripture is clear: you are no mistake. Jesus did not bleed and die for a mistake. Ephesians 1:4 says, "He chose us in him before the creation of the world to be holy and blameless in his sight" (NIV).

The Lord had you on his mind long before you were even an inkling in the minds of your parents. As you think about the detail of creation, how a human being is formed by the joining of one sperm and one egg, do you really believe that God does anything accidentally? Before he placed the pillars of this world, he laid out what color skin you would have, where you would live, who your parents would be, if you would have dark hair, if you would have light eyes. You are composed of the exact, God-ordained DNA needed to make a custom-made you!

In order to believe God, you must embrace the truth that he does not make mistakes and that your birth was no accident. Scripture says, "Through him God created everything in the heavenly realms and on earth. He made the things we can see and the things we can't see—such as thrones, kingdoms, rulers, and authorities in the unseen world. Everything was created through him and for him" (Colossians 1:16). What a concept! Now if we could just let this truth penetrate deep into our inner beings.

God's motivation for creating you was love, and his focus was designing an earth you could inhabit and reside in as the most valuable of his entire creation! Don't you think God could have chosen to exist eternally in a pre-earth state if he so desired? Of course he could have. But instead he breathed a universe into being. He desired to have a place for us to live in order for him to show his love to his children. God made you so he could love you!

Do you doubt your worth today? Do you believe the lie that

your existence here on this earth is a fluke, that your birth is a mere accident? No matter what anyone else says, your Creator says that you are "fearfully and wonderfully made" (Psalm 139:14, NIV).

You Are His Delight

Not only were you formed completely on purpose, but you were also made to the very delight of God. You exist to bring joy and pleasure to your Lord. The book of Revelation says that all of creation—us included—was made for one reason: to give glory to God: "You are worthy, O Lord our God, to receive glory and honor and power. For you created all things, and they exist because you created what you pleased" (Revelation 4:11).

It may seem strange to think about, but did you know that God feels things—that he has emotions, just as we do?

> He gets jealous from time to time (see 2 Corinthians 11:2).
> He gets angry (see Psalm 7:11).
> He can grieve (see Ephesians 4:30).
> He feels pity and compassion (see Judges 2:18).
> And perhaps most striking of all, the Bible is clear
>   that he delights in us and feels love toward us
>   (see 2 Chronicles 9:8; Zephaniah 3:17).

It can be easy for us to feel small and insignificant in the eyes of the Lord. When most people picture the almighty God, they tend to envision a giant grandfather figure. You know, an older man, aged with wisdom, sporting a white beard and white hair, sitting on a huge throne holding a scepter—which apparently is used to send lightning bolts from heaven to strike us if we mess up really bad! So many people, even Christians, have a skewed view of who God really is. Yes, he is mighty. Yes, he is all-powerful. And yes, if he so desired, he could strike us down with a heavenly lightning bolt. But he is also a loving, compassionate Father who is patient with us, "not wanting anyone to perish" (2 Peter 3:9, NIV). He created you intentionally, and you are his delight!

Now, how are you going to take these truths and allow them to transform your present reality? If you are beginning to truly believe that God delights in you, and if your heart's desire is to please him, you must embrace the words of 2 Corinthians 5:9: "Our goal is to please him." You must make God himself your goal. That means that your life must be a continual act of worship and surrender to your Father—a living sacrifice—just as he delights in you and sacrificed for you.

YOU ARE NAMED BY GOD: *You are his delight.*

CHAPTER 13

Seizing His Plan For You

I CAN'T TELL YOU how many times I've decided I'll never understand why something took place in my life, and then eventually I find myself standing smack-dab in a lightbulb moment. One of those moments came on a windy spring evening on a campus park bench while I was waiting for my long night of grad school classes to begin.

As an older student who stayed in school because I had no clue what I wanted to do after college graduation, I had made it a point to befriend some of the younger students on campus who attended my church. Most of them were freshmen and sophomores, and I enjoyed showing them around the college grounds, helping them find their classes, and just loving on them during this sometimes scary season of life.

One freshman girl (we'll call her Kelly) came straight from

the country to what she considered the big city. I couldn't bring myself to tell her that thirty-five thousand people hardly qualified as a big city, but compared to her town of fifteen hundred, maybe it was.

I liked Kelly immediately. She was outgoing and funny. I could also tell she was covering up her fear and insecurity with her attempts to be the center of attention (a defense mechanism I have to admit we had in common). Kelly and I crossed paths several times a week during the spring semester. If time allowed, we would chat on the bench outside our building before classes began.

On one evening in particular, I knew something was wrong the moment I sat down next to her. It was obvious she had been crying, and it seemed like she had just been waiting for someone to come along and listen. The moment I touched her arm, she began pouring out her tragedy to me through uncontrollable sobs.

Kelly told me she had been the victim of a date rape the night before, and she felt as if her world was caving in. We both missed our classes as she replayed every horrifying detail from the night before. I listened, rubbed her back, handed her tissues, and cried right along with her. As she began to wrap up her story, she paused and attempted to gain control of her sobs through deep, broken breaths of air.

For what seemed like an eternity we both just sat on the bench in silence. Finally Kelly collected herself enough to say, "How will any good Christian man ever want me? Why would God let this happen?"

And there it was—my own personal lightbulb moment.

This girl was me, only eight years before.

This is where I start to get a glimpse into the workings of the

Almighty. "Wow. So this is how you will use that awful situation in my life for your glory?" And there on a campus bench, on an otherwise ordinary evening, I got the honor of wiping a girl's tear-stained cheeks, looking straight into her eyes, and saying, "Oh, honey, does he have a plan for you! And this is how I know. . . ."

When God Throws You a Curveball

One thing my family and friends know about me is this: I'm a planner! I thrive on lists and calendars (preferably color coded, with bullet points). I attempt to arrange everything in my day down to the smallest detail. But what God has been teaching me is that he doesn't operate based on *my* plans! I have no way of seeing into the days that lie before me. I can't predict what the Lord's plan for my life will look like, and I certainly can't control it. I just have to trust my future to him. Even when I can see how God has worked in my life in the past, it doesn't give me a guarantee about how he'll work in my future. The truth is, just when we think we've got God all figured out, he just might decide to throw us a curveball!

When I was in graduate school, I was in my prime of obsessive-compulsive planning. I was married and getting my master's degree in community counseling. My husband was happy, I was happy, and I had our future all planned out—complete with bullet points and highlights. My list looked something like this:

- Justin would continue in his job, which he enjoyed and felt God had called him to.
- I would graduate and continue to work toward my counseling license.

- I would then, most assuredly, hire on with some amazing community counseling clinic, where I would inevitably be overwhelmed with clients.
- On the side, I would finish my online seminary degree in order to satisfy my desire to go into full-time church ministry someday.

Sounds like a great plan, right?

Except that I ended up walking across the stage to receive my degree with some slightly different circumstances than I'd expected. As I trotted proudly across the platform in three-inch red heels, not even my puffy black graduation gown could cover up my seven-months-pregnant belly! It didn't take long before my color-coded, bullet-pointed list was scattered, drooled on, and stomped on by the new little addition to our family.

That was only the beginning of how God's plans started diverging from mine. Now, several years (and another drooler) later, I am still finding pieces of highlighted paper here and there—under the bed, taped to the fridge, between the couch cushions. I guess I'm still learning my lesson!

It goes without saying that nowhere in my neat list of life plans did I intend to enter public ministry after spending time in the pit. If someone had mentioned the idea to me back then, I'd have declared her certifiably crazy. As if I wanted to stand in front of people and tell my story! And besides, I was convinced that no one would listen. (God and I are laughing together as I write these words.)

I don't know exactly what God has in mind for my own life, let alone for yours. However, if we can start believing what we *do* know of God's plan for us, we will soon find that the parts we don't know really don't matter all that much anymore. In order to take yet another step in transforming our present, we must *presently* believe in God's ultimate plan for our lives.

In my years of following Christ, I have come to the conclusion that many Christians make finding God's present will for us way too complex. We wrongly believe that it's only possible for the most talented and the most gifted and the most spiritual to know the heart of God. But in reality, it's much simpler than that. If we long to see God at work in our present, we merely need to grow in our daily longing for him.

In recent years I've come to realize that spiritual growth is not so much a to-do list or an attempt to master the external mechanics of Christian living. It's more about humbly placing ourselves before God in order to be changed. I have tasted the true liberation of basking in the sheer privilege of having access to the Lord of lords, and I'm never going back. The daily privileges that go along with this include reading and meditating on God's Word, communicating with the Lord through continual conversations with him (otherwise known as prayer), daily confession of my fleshly desires, repentance, service to my family and the church body, and corporate worship.

> In order to take another step in transforming our present, we must *presently* believe in God's ultimate plan for our lives.

These are privileges we must intentionally pursue each day. And trust me, the reward is greater than any sacrifice you might make. "Give, and you will receive. Your gift will return to you in full—pressed down, shaken together to make room for more, running over, and poured into your lap. The amount you give will determine the amount you get back" (Luke 6:38).

All Things for Good

Trust me, friend, God's plan for your life is far better than anything you have thought up or imagined. His purpose is twofold: to bring you good and to bring him glory. The following passage from Scripture is packed with truths about what God has designed for our future:

> We know that in all things God works for the good of those who love him, who have been called according to his purpose. For those God foreknew he also predestined to be conformed to the image of his Son, that he might be the firstborn among many brothers and sisters. And those he predestined, he also called; those he called, he also justified; those he justified, he also glorified. ROMANS 8:28-30 (NIV)

All: God is working in every area of your life, not just in isolated situations. He cares about each detail. There is nothing too little or too big for God to handle. Case in point: have you ever consulted God before you made a phone call or had a conversation with someone? Whether it's a brief chat with a cubicle-mate or a lengthy talk with Great-Aunt Melba, whom you haven't seen in years, do you ask God to work through you in that conversation? Maybe you assume that God doesn't care about such tiny details of your life. Oh, but he does! He cares about *all* things that take place in the lives of his children. He has also delicately orchestrated the grand, overarching themes of your life. He cares about if and whom you will marry, how you will influence the next generation, and how you will use the gifts and abilities he has given you to minister to your family, friends, coworkers, and church family. He has appointed all the details in your life, large and small, just as he did for Jeremiah:

> The Lord replied, "Don't say, 'I'm too young,' for you must go wherever I send you and say whatever I tell you. And don't be afraid of the people, for I will be with you and will protect you. I, the Lord, have spoken!" Then the Lord reached out and touched my mouth and said,
> "Look, I have put my words in your mouth!
> Today I appoint you to stand up against nations and kingdoms.
> Some you must uproot and tear down, destroy and overthrow.
> Others you must build up and plant." JEREMIAH 1:7-10

Good: When God states that he is working for your good, it doesn't mean that everything that happens in your life *will* be good. He is looking at a bigger picture than we are—our eternal future. He is working out his good in your life to bring you into a closer relationship with him. Bad things happen because evil has invaded every corner of our fallen world, but God can work good out of even the worst situations. God isn't always working to make you happy, but he is constantly moving toward completing his ultimate purpose: making you into a more accurate image bearer of his Son, Jesus Christ.

Those God foreknew: It is important to note here that God's promise of good does not apply to everyone. This promise can be fulfilled only for those who love him, who have been "called according to his purpose." The called ones are those who have heeded the burning of the Holy Spirit within them. They are the reborn, the saved, the beautiful ones who have responded and accepted the call of Christ (see Acts 2:38-39).

Predestined: To be predestined is another way of saying that God has known you all along. Before the foundations of the world, God set a plan in place for you, a calling designed specifically for you, and he knew you would be one of his chosen creations who would accept him and believe in him (see Ephesians 1:5, 11).

Likeness: God's ultimate plan for your life is revealed here—to be made into the very likeness of his Son. As my old youth pastor would say, "We need to be running around this earth like little Jesuses!" The interesting thing about being a mirror of Christ is that the closer you get to becoming like Christ, the closer you get to being your true self! And the closer you get to your true self, the more evident God's plan is for your life.

> God isn't always working to make you happy, but he is constantly moving toward completing his ultimate purpose: making you into a more accurate image bearer of his Son, Jesus Christ.

Called: *Called* literally means to be summoned or invited. Take a look at 2 Thessalonians 2:14: "[God] called you to salvation when we told you the Good News; now you can share in the glory of our Lord Jesus Christ." This verse is a bold reminder of the very essence of being called by God. When you begin to doubt your worth and question your existence, remember that you were invited to take part in fellowship with him. There is nothing you did or can do to earn this calling. It is like receiving a birthday invitation in the mail. You were invited to the birthday party because the host desired your presence. (And the great thing about God's party is that you're not required to bring a gift!)

Justified: Justification is the act or state of being declared right with God. Being justified means that God declares you not guilty for the sins you have committed in the past and will commit in the future. He is essentially saying that no matter what you do, he has already stamped you as accepted and loved in his book. Don't get me wrong, this is not a pass card to sin whenever you desire, but this *is* a get-out-of-hell-free card (see Romans 5:1-2 and Titus 3:5-7, NIV).

Glorified: The Bible says that someday believers' physical bodies will reach a glorified state, although this is not something we will necessarily behold in this lifetime (see 1 Corinthians 15:42-53). Once we have breathed our last of this worldly air and inhaled the beautiful aroma of eternity, full glorification will commence. This is the state when the believer becomes fully like Christ. For now, however, we can get a glimpse of God's glory within us. In Jesus' final prayer on earth, he says, "I have given [my followers] the glory that you gave me, that they may be one as we are one—I in them and you in me—so that they may be brought to complete unity" (John 17:22-23, NIV).

God's glory dwells within all believers, no matter how unglorified you may think your outside looks. As you embrace your purpose in the Lord, the glory within you begins to grow and reveal itself through your speech and actions. You should live not to bring yourself glory but to glorify God and let others see the Lord working through you: "Let your light shine before others, that they may see your good deeds and glorify your Father in heaven" (Matthew 5:16, NIV).

• • •

Are the puzzle pieces beginning to come together? Are you beginning to believe all that God has in store for you? Once you let it sink in that God has a good plan for you *right now*, you will begin to see a total transformation of your present condition. As the past hurts begin to heal, they will gradually begin to fade into distant shadows, leaving you to face today. And your future depends on your current belief system.

There are no man-made lists that could come close to standing up against the plans your Father has written down for you on his heavenly tablet.

I have an assignment for you right now. Take your list of life plans, wad it up as tightly as you can, walk over to the trash can, and chuck it in. It doesn't matter how detailed your plan was or how long and hard you worked to compose its contents. Throw it away! Trust me, there are no man-made lists that could come close to standing up against the plans your Father has written down for you on his heavenly tablet. In my mind, I picture the Creator God using one hand to reach out and form a majestic mountaintop and the other hand to hold a notepad with your name on it. Oh, and I don't think it was just a blank piece of paper—it was no doubt highlighted with hues of color yet to be seen by the human eye and bullet-pointed with the stars! "'I know the plans I have for you,' declares the LORD, 'plans to prosper you and not to harm you, plans to give you hope and a future'" (Jeremiah 29:11, NIV).

So now we know that God has redeemed our past and that he is in the business of transforming our present. We know that he has called us and chosen us for a purpose that is beyond anything we can imagine. But how do we get there? How can we embrace an audacious faith that brings us into an adventure-packed future of hope, joy, and power? Stay with me in this, friend, because that's what part 3 is all about!

> YOU ARE NAMED BY GOD: *You are chosen.*

Part 3

Embracing Your Future

BY THE GRACE OF GOD, we as believers no longer have to live as slaves to the mistakes and pain of our past. Our present has been transformed, and we can now look toward the future with hope. Even as we look forward, however, our thorns stay with us. The apostle Paul had his own thorn: "To keep me from becoming proud, I was given a thorn in my flesh, a messenger from Satan to torment me and keep me from becoming proud" (2 Corinthians 12:7).

I don't know what Paul's thorn was, but I'm all too familiar with my own. My thorn is the people I've hurt over the years. For the rest of my life, I will remember the faces of those I've wounded and the pain I've caused them. That thorn remains in my flesh as a devastating reminder of what I am capable of doing outside the Lord's will. I no longer pray that God will release me from the backlash of my poor choices. Now I think, *Paul had a thorn—why shouldn't I?*

Perhaps your thorn is more physical in makeup—a chronic pain in your knee or your neck, or headaches that never cease. Maybe your thorn is a nagging repercussion from your own poor choice from long ago, or maybe it's a financial situation, a strained relationship, or a compulsion to pick up that bottle or pop that pill. Perhaps your thorn is your memories—those times when a thought, a smell, or a song takes you back to a place in time you never wish to return to.

As painful as they are, our thorns keep us humble. They remind us of the places we should never venture again and the people we once were and should never again desire to be. But as we look toward embracing the future God has for us, we need to remember that our thorns are intended to keep us humble and continually turn us back to God, not to hold us in captivity.

It is only when we have surrendered ourselves to God that he can plant a vision inside us. In his mysterious, redemptive ways, God can take the broken pieces of our past and the transformed pieces of our present and weave them together into a beautiful calling for our future.

The theme verses for my life are the same as my "brother" David's:

> Purify me from my sins, and I will be clean;
>> wash me, and I will be whiter than snow.
> Oh, give me back my joy again;
>> you have broken me—
>> now let me rejoice.
> Don't keep looking at my sins.
>> Remove the stain of my guilt.

Create in me a clean heart, O God.
> Renew a loyal spirit within me.
Do not banish me from your presence,
> and don't take your Holy Spirit from me.

Restore to me the joy of your salvation,
> and make me willing to obey you.
Then I will teach your ways to rebels,
> and they will return to you. PSALM 51:7-13

God has purified me, removed my guilt, cleaned my heart, and restored my joy. And now he has given me the calling to be a teacher and to share the redemptive work he has done in my life. And so I dare to live each day as one called by God. Yes, my thorns are in tow, but they are now only brilliant reminders of my new-found, condemnation-free life in Jesus Christ.

If I could, I'd reach outside the pages of this book and squeeze your little cheeks into submission as I looked you in the eyes. I'd say to you, "Listen to me, dear one. If he can give me a calling for the future, he can certainly do the same for you."

CHAPTER 14

Dare to Live

AS WE EMBARK ON THIS FINAL SECTION TOGETHER, I'd like to take this opportunity to introduce you to one of the most remarkable people I've ever had the privilege of knowing. Throughout my quest of passionately and courageously pursuing Christ, this person has come alongside me as my mentor and my guide. He has encouraged me, blessed me, and challenged me to get intimate with my Creator. He is one of the boldest and most fearless Christ followers I have ever encountered.

Please don't misunderstand—my friend is not perfect. He struggles with the flesh on a continual basis, just like I do. And just like me, he has a past that isn't much to be proud of. In fact, the only good things either of us can glean from our past have nothing to do with us and everything to do with what Christ has done for us.

God Almighty reached down into both our lives, got his hands covered in our filth, made some major adjustments here and there, scrubbed us up a bit, and voilà! Now we both have stories of radical transformation—of being completely forgiven and made sparkling clean. Praise God for his ability to bring about total change!

God was able to take two hypocritical, immature, self-absorbed individuals and bring us through a time of refining, which then gave birth to new, God-glorifying creations. Here is another area in which my friend and I relate. We both desire to live out the time in our refined bodies with bold, fearless abandon. With each breath, we long to push our limits in order to give God glory and make him known to every individual we come into contact with. My friend has been an example and an inspiration to me in these areas.

My one disappointment is that I've never actually had the privilege of meeting my friend face-to-face. He has been in the presence of our Father for a while now. Regardless, I feel as though we are connected beyond time and space. When I read his words on paper, I feel as though he is speaking directly to me. Among the many personalities and voices I have come across on the pages of Scripture, there is one with whom my bond runs deepest: Paul.

I first met Paul in the seventh chapter of the book of Acts, although at that point he was actually going by the name Saul. When I first approached him, he was not someone I envisioned spending much time getting to know. My attention was initially drawn to him as he stood amid a group of rowdy, furious Jewish leaders. As the crowd grew larger and louder, the self-righteous Saul looked on, condoning and encouraging the murderous pack of religious bigots.

The crowd was clustering around a young Christ follower

named Stephen, a man who had been anointed by God to preach to the Jews about Christ. While addressing the Jews, Stephen did the thing that tends to push people's buttons when it comes to issues of faith—he made it personal. Stephen called the assembly out on their sin and their misunderstanding of their spiritual roots. People will go to extreme measures to avoid feeling convicted, and this case was no exception. The religious leaders went so far as to stone Stephen to death!

There's no doubt that Saul had his own buttons pushed that day too. Not only did he give his approval for the stoning of Stephen, but he held the people's clothes as they shed their layers to throw stones at this messenger of God. Saul watched in support as they dragged Stephen out of the city and threw stone after stone at him until he breathed his last (see Acts 7:54-60).

For better or worse, Saul and I share a similar personality characteristic—we are passionate. We don't ride the fence or do things halfway. When that passion is focused on furthering Christ's Kingdom, it can be a beneficial trait. But when it is focused on anything the flesh desires, oh . . . it is not pretty! When we first hear about Saul in Scripture, he has committed his life to the passionate pursuit of destroying the church of God. He goes from house to house throughout the land, dragging off any man or woman who professes to be a Christian and throwing them in prison.

But God has another plan for Saul. And it is at the lowest and most sin-filled moment of Saul's life that God gets his attention in a profound way.

Saul has just received permission from the high priest to travel 150 miles to Damascus to search out anyone who is a follower of Christ. Saul is a driven man as he sets out toward Damascus.

I doubt he allows his companions much time to sleep or eat on the road, as all he can think about is placing those believers in chains and dragging them back to a filthy, dark pit in a Jerusalem prison. But as Saul nears the city gates of Damascus, something extraordinary happens. A brilliant light from heaven floods the road around Saul and his companions. Instantly Saul becomes one of the most blessed creatures of all time as his ears are filled with the audible voice of the Lord. I'm pretty sure the ring of Jesus' voice would break even the coldest of hearts—and it most assuredly breaks Saul's. The Lord blinds Saul for three days as he works in the heart of his "chosen instrument" (see Acts 9:1-19).

After a few days of fellowship with other believers, a bit of food, and some recharging, Saul wastes no time spreading the name of the Lord. As the Lord sends Saul out with a calling and a completely transformed vision for his future (despite his past, mind you), Saul also gets a new name—Paul (see Acts 13). The internal changes God has worked in him are reflected by his new identity.

Paul not only emerges as a new man with a new name, but he is also an apostle of the living God with a clear purpose: to bring glory to Christ. Paul's life is a brilliant example of what can be in store for any of us who choose a future surrendered to Christ over the chains of the past.

Paul's life is utterly transformed that day. Changed from persecutor to preacher, Paul eventually goes on to take the gospel of Christ to the Roman Empire. He lives as a man on a mission. He is still passionate, still bold, but his focus is now set on the prize. He is running a new race with new teammates. If there was ever a radical Christian, Paul is it!

Before the foundations of the world were laid, God knew that he would use every piece of Paul's filthy past for God's own glory. Paul's background, his training, his citizenship, and even his weaknesses prepared him for the greatest and most rewarding challenge of his life—his calling to bring the gospel to the world. God uses Paul's transformation not only to rock Paul's life but also to rock the lives of everyone Paul would come in contact with—and countless generations after him.

Christ desires to work the same kind of transformation within you! He has given you a new name and a new purpose. The question is—are you willing to be *rocked*?

The Road to Maturity

As days turn into months and months turn into years, we naturally find ourselves growing older—with no extra energy needed on our part. Aging is simply a natural biological progression. Maturity, on the other hand, isn't so automatic. Becoming mature in a particular area of our lives takes intentional pursuit.

If we are going to be overcomers in this world and not the overcome, it is essential that we mature in Christ. This can't just be a side hobby or something we do when we have some extra time; it must become our daily reason for living. No matter how old we are or how many years we have been going to church or have been Christians, we never arrive at the summit of spiritual maturity. There is always a need to step up our game when it comes to pursuing Christ and showing him to those around us.

No matter what the season in our lives—whether things are smooth sailing or we're up against some rough waters—Jesus Christ has summoned us to stand firm to the end. If we long to be audacious Christ followers, it simply isn't an option for us to disconnect from God and his people. This isn't something that comes naturally at first, but we have to make a conscious choice every day to grow. It's kind of like riding a bike. We're not born with the natural ability to hop on and start pedaling, but with time and practice, we can become quite proficient (or mature) at riding. Eventually the process becomes more natural.

Maturity is about a choice—a commitment. And there are no shortcuts to maturity. The only way to get there is through the intentional process of discipleship. It requires a day-by-day effort to become more like Christ in everything we do. Here are a few take-home definitions for you:

Maturity: being fully developed—physically, mentally, emotionally, and spiritually

Discipleship: the process of becoming like Christ

Maturity and discipleship work hand in hand. At the heart of both lies the necessity of change. Paul paints a picture for us of what it will be like when we are "mature in the Lord, measuring up to the full and complete standard of Christ" (Ephesians 4:13). He goes on to say:

> Then we will no longer be immature like children. We won't be tossed and blown about by every wind of new teaching. We will not be influenced when people try to trick us with lies so clever they sound like the truth. Instead, we will speak the truth in love, growing in every way more and more like Christ, who is the head of his body, the church. He makes the whole body

fit together perfectly. As each part does its own special work, it helps the other parts grow, so that the whole body is healthy and growing and full of love. With the Lord's authority I say this: Live no longer as the Gentiles do, for they are hopelessly confused. EPHESIANS 4:14-17

The direction for biblical maturity is clear: don't live the same way you once did. As Christians, our maturity depends on whether we choose to resemble Christ or the rest of the world.

As a Bible study teacher, I am occasionally approached by people who are struggling with spiritual complacency or the genuineness of their salvation. When this happens, I ask them to perform a simple assessment of their life pre-Christ and post-Christ. I ask them to go home and literally put pen to paper. In one column I tell them to write down a list of thoughts and behaviors they engaged in before they came to know the Lord. In another column, they list thoughts and behaviors they have engaged in since coming to know the Lord. If there is very little difference between the two columns, it's likely we're seeing a lack of maturity.

> Maturity is about a choice—a commitment. And there are no shortcuts to maturity.

If other people can't tell the difference in the way you dress, the places you go, the friends you hang out with, the activities you take part in, and the way you speak now that you are a Christian, it very well may be because you are not maturing in your relationship with the Lord. You are not, in other words, growing up. You're still wearing diapers in the nursery while everyone else is outside on the playground in their "big girl" underwear.

Jesus makes it clear in Scripture that the path to maturity is not an easy one. He tells his disciples, "If any of you wants to be my follower, you must turn from your selfish ways, take up your cross, and follow me" (Matthew 16:24). There is only one way for us to become true disciples of Christ, and that is through dying to self—surrendering each day what we think we know and what we desire to the hand and will of God. We must make a choice to leave everything behind and follow him. In order to drive this point home, let's take a few moments to look at a man named Matthew—a disciple of Christ who is best known for writing the book of Matthew in the Bible.

Here's where his story begins: "As Jesus was walking along, he saw a man named Matthew sitting at his tax collector's booth. 'Follow me and be my disciple,' Jesus said to him. So Matthew got up and followed him" (Matthew 9:9). We need to make a special note about Matthew here. As a tax collector, he's despised by his people because of his profession. Matthew is a Jew appointed by the Romans to collect taxes from his fellow Jews. It was common practice for tax collectors in his day to take a commission on what they collected, and on top of that, most overcharged their fellow citizens and kept the profit for themselves. So believe me when I say he's not a popular guy.

When Jesus looks at Matthew sitting there and says, "Follow me," Matthew is faced with a choice. He can stay right there, seated with the sinners, and continue making money through his lucrative career, or he can get up from his chair, abandon his tax collector buddies, and sacrifice his money and his lifestyle to follow Christ. We know very little about Matthew himself, which is one of the reasons I love him—he is serious about making his account all about Christ and not at all about himself. But what we do know of Matthew is quite enough—God chooses him, inspiring him by the Holy Spirit, to write the first Gospel.

The book of Matthew serves as the perfect bridge between the Old Testament, which is a book of God's promises, and the New Testament, which is a book of God's fulfillment of those promises. Matthew's Gospel is the first to emphasize the crossover from promise to fulfillment, and because Matthew makes the monumental choice to change, he goes down in history as a visionary who brought the past into a present reality.

As Matthew would tell you, becoming a disciple of Christ is a daily commitment. Commitments shape our lives. Commitments make us or break us.

A commitment to Christ is a lot like a marriage commitment, in that it requires a daily promise to work at the relationship. In my relationship with Justin, what if I had said, "I do," but then refused to change from that wide-eyed, passion-pumped twenty-two-year-old girl? What if I'd never moved on or made the choice to grow as a person and as a wife? Well, I don't think I have to tell you that that would be a divorce waiting to happen. Marriage is not a one-time decision; it's something we wake up and commit to every day. A commitment to Christ is the same idea—in fact, Jesus talks a lot about the daily aspect of the Christian life: "If any of you wants to be my follower, you must turn from your selfish ways, take up your cross *daily*, and follow me" (Luke 9:23, emphasis added). And in teaching us to pray, he says, "Give us *each day* the food we need" (Luke 11:3, emphasis added).

Jesus knows our human tendency to get overwhelmed and give up; therefore, he insists that while we do make an initial commitment to change and grow, we do so on a daily basis. If we try to skip steps because we are anxious to be grown up already, we will inevitably give up. We want to see the change happen overnight, but what we don't realize is that the change can't happen without the struggle.

Complete Transformation

So what, exactly, does God ask of us? In a word, everything.

Jesus says in Luke 14:26-27, "If anyone comes to me and does not hate father and mother, wife and children, brothers and sisters—yes, even their own life—such a person cannot be my disciple. And whoever does not carry their cross and follow me cannot be my disciple" (NIV). Those are tough words to swallow. Even so, I believe this passage is beautiful—not only because the words are spoken by the "God made flesh" himself, but also because they teach us exactly what it takes to become a true disciple of Christ.

The word *hate* in this verse does not suggest a sinful disposition or an instruction to mistreat others. Rather, it means "to love less." Our love for Christ must be supreme. We must love Christ more than our own flesh and blood and more than our own lives. Our love for Christ must be so intense that all other love is like hatred in comparison.

And what does it mean to carry our cross? Jesus is talking about complete devotion to the Lord—even to the point of dying to ourselves. We must be willing to surrender our own ambitions, our own plans, our own rights, and be willing to serve him no matter the cost.

In light of this passage, let me ask you a few tough questions. What specifically needs to change in your life today in order for you to more faithfully carry your cross? What addictions, thoughts, attitudes, activities, or people are hindering you from complete discipleship? If you are finding it difficult to unload your arms in order to have room to pick up your cross, think for a moment about Jesus. He gave up everything—his spot in heaven, his unbroken fellowship with the Father—to carry his cross for *you*. How could we do any less?

And here's the thing about carrying our cross: it's the only way true transformation is possible in our lives. When we become cross-bearing disciples of Christ, it's not only our insides that are renewed but our outsides as well. That's right—our actions and appearance start looking a little more like Christ's with each committed day that passes. "All of us who have had that veil removed can see and reflect the glory of the Lord. And the Lord—who is the Spirit—makes us more and more like him as we are changed into his glorious image" (2 Corinthians 3:18).

Oh, to be Christians who radiate the glory of the Lord! That is my heart's desire, and I pray it is yours as well. I long for us to be people of such radiant beauty that we literally stop people in their tracks! I want to be in the line of people throughout history who have been radically transformed by God.

- Abraham: from idolater to the father of God's people (see Genesis 12–25)

- Joseph: from dreamer to ruler (see Genesis 37–50)
- Moses: from insecure runaway to deliverer (see Exodus 2–Joshua 1)
- David: from adulterer to God's beloved (see 1 Samuel 16–1 Kings 2)
- Job: from overwhelmed to restored (see the book of Job)
- Jeremiah: from doubter to dynamic voice of the Lord (see the book of Jeremiah)
- Jonah: from fearful to obedient (see the book of Jonah)
- Matthew: from sinner to disciple (see Matthew 9:9)
- Paul: from murderer to apostle (see Acts 9:1-19)
- [Your name] _____: from _____ to _____

Once we've committed to living transformed lives, how do we begin this process? Scripture gives us this blueprint: "Do not conform to the pattern of this world, but be transformed by the renewing of your mind" (Romans 12:2, NIV). The transformation of both our internal character and external actions begins with the renewal of our minds (and here I thought it was the tanning bed and self-help books!). Here's a quick definition for you:

Transformed: to be changed in appearance or character

So if the key to complete transformation is our minds, the next question is, How do we renew our minds? The answer is simple, but it's not always easy. Renewal of the mind depends on what information goes into it. Think of it this way: What TV shows and movies do you watch? What do you read? What do you listen to? What do you look at online? Any information your mind processes will contribute to your ability to be transformed . . . or not.

When I was growing up, I remember my mom and dad telling me, "You *are* who you hang around with." I didn't necessarily like their comment at the time, but now I recognize there is much truth to it. And the same goes for *what* we hang around with. You don't need me to tell you that in today's culture we are inundated with sex, lies, and scandal from every direction. We need only turn on the television to receive a strong dose of this fallen world. It is not enough just to be a "good person" who lives a good life. If we desire to be completely transformed into the visible image of the Savior, we must be on constant guard about what goes into our minds.

Put Up a Good Defense System

If you were to record every thought that went through your mind in a given day, what would you find? What is your mind set on? In the book of Philippians, Paul paints a picture of those who are not living a life worthy of Christ's calling: "Their destiny is destruction, their god is their stomach, and their glory is in their shame. Their mind is set on earthly things" (3:19, NIV). This is a sobering description of people who are concerned only about feeding their selfish appetites.

It's not enough to stop those old bad habits—now you need to replace them with godly behaviors.

Let me update this a bit for you. If the party is at a bar where everyone is getting hammered, these people go and join the party. If the gang is headed to a tasteless R-rated movie, these people tag along without a care. If sex is what everyone else in the group is doing, these people join in to be cool. Simply put, their minds are on "earthly things."

Maybe you are shaking your head in disgust right now, thinking you're above such things. If that's the case, let's bring this a little closer to home. Maybe the week has been so busy for you that when Sunday comes, you skip worship to get some extra sleep. Or maybe you make it to church every Sunday, but during the message you tune out what the preacher is saying and start doodling a list of restaurants you'd like to head to after the service. Maybe you feel the nudge to crack open your Bible or talk to God during the evening, but then you remember your favorite TV show is on and you promise to do it tomorrow instead.

If you are only looking for change that is easy or convenient, stop reading here. But if you are looking to be sold out for God and live a life of passionately pursuing him, then this part is for you. Colossians 3:2 commands us, "Set your minds on things above, not on earthly things" (NIV). One of the best ways to keep our minds on things above is to keep the things of this world (such as materialism, illicit sex, and self-indulgence) out.

When I am teaching, I often pose this question to the audience: "Are you currently living in a way that you would have no shame in being there, saying that, or thinking that if Christ returned right that moment?" When we begin to think of life on the other side of death, this temporary existence seems brief and insignificant in comparison. When we learn to see things through the filter of God's perspective, we begin to love like he loves; we begin to desire the things he desires. Suddenly, that sitcom just isn't as funny as it once was, the mindless magazine isn't as engaging, the online shopping doesn't have the same pull.

If we want to put up a good defense system, we need to intentionally structure our lives for change. In many cases, change requires drastic action. If you want to be delivered from smoking, stop going to stores that sell cigarettes. If you want to stop looking at pornography and engaging in self-gratification, move the computer into a more public location—or remove it altogether. If you wish to be free of your bad temper and foul mouth, stop hanging out with people who lose their cool and cuss like a sailor. If you don't want to feel defeated and insecure, stop spending all your time on social networking sites and the telephone.

Putting up a mental defense system requires two steps. First, you must make whatever sacrifice is needed to distance yourself from your old nature. Your activities, your surroundings, and your relationships must be consistent with your desire to put off sin. Scripture leaves no gray area here: "Don't be fooled by those who say such things, for 'bad company corrupts good character.' Think carefully about what is right, and stop sinning" (1 Corinthians 15:33-34).

The second step is to take the space you cleared from your old ways and fill it with things that help you grow in your maturity with the Lord. It's not enough to stop those old bad habits—now you need to replace them with godly behaviors. For instance, maybe your old way was to speak harshly to others. It's not enough to curb your temper; you also need to learn a new way of communicating. "A gentle answer deflects anger, but harsh words make tempers flare" (Proverbs 15:1). Or maybe you have a tendency to take what doesn't belong to you, whether that's time, money, or resources. Scripture says we need to not only stop that behavior but replace it with generosity. "If you are a thief, quit stealing.

Instead, use your hands for good hard work, and then give generously to others in need" (Ephesians 4:28).

Fill Your Mind with the Word

If we want our minds to be transformed, it is absolutely essential that we immerse ourselves in the Word of God.

You want to know when I experienced my personal time of mind renewal? It was the moment I stopped treating my Bible like a book of stories and started viewing it as the very breath of my Creator. Transformation took place in my life when I allowed the Word of God to take root in my bones, when I allowed it to give life to every organ and blood-pumping vein in my body!

The living Word of God is not just any tool but the tool we must use on a daily basis to keep our minds focused and renewed. It has the power to refine us and break us when we need to change. "'Does not my word burn like fire?' says the LORD. 'Is it not like a mighty hammer that smashes a rock to pieces?'" (Jeremiah 23:29).

Please let go of the notion that the Bible is nothing but a book of Sunday school stories or a doctrinal guidebook. Oh, it is so much more! It is our source of power. It can infuse life into our weak and feeble bodies. It is the Bread of Life—the food we need on a daily basis to keep us alive. Unfortunately, many Christians today are starving and in desperate need of spiritual nourishment.

Most of us have heard that the Bible is important. We've even read the familiar verse in 2 Timothy: "All Scripture is God-breathed and is useful for teaching, rebuking, correcting and training in righteousness" (3:16, NIV). Why, then, do we use it so little? For many years of my Christian life, I staggered along, believing *in* my Bible. I would carry it with me to church on Sunday and even open it a time or two when I really needed some encourage-ment or uplifting words. I believed the Bible was truth, yet I had never taken the time to read it from cover to cover. I spent years devoting time to other activities—going out to eat, taking the kids to school, hanging out with friends, watching television, talking on the phone—yet my Bible sat there closed, day after day. No pages turned, no truths felt, no notes made, and definitely no transformation.

The Word of God is our life support! How long do we really think we will last when we're taken off life support? Yes, our bod-ies will continue to function, but our minds and hearts will begin gasping for breath, fading . . . fading . . . fading . . . until we flatline.

Praise God that he has brought me to a place now where my heart thrills at the sound of the crisp-turning pages of Scripture. This didn't happen overnight, though. Like any new diet or work-out program, this takes time to become a habit, and it's not easy. There are days we don't feel like getting on the treadmill or eating healthily, and there will be days when we don't feel like reading the Bible. But trust me, the payoff is worth it. Digging into God's Word involves a beautiful dance between love and discipline—the two go hand in hand. The more disciplined you are, the more you will learn to love God's Word. And the more you love God's Word, the more disciplined you will be.

If you want to read the Bible but you're not sure where to begin, I suggest beginning with a Bible study guide to set up the daily reading assignments for you. I also recommend that you include a trustworthy Bible commentary alongside your Bible to help you understand what you're reading. It's helpful to understand the context surrounding the passages, and there is no better way to be enlightened than through the wise instruction of teachers who have gone before us. And if you're looking for a spot to start, I suggest that you get to know the "boys" well—the Gospels of Matthew, Mark, Luke, and John.

Oh, favored one of the King, believe that he is bigger than you ever imagined. Be prepared to be changed from the inside out! Your life will never be the same.

YOU ARE NAMED BY GOD: *You are transformed.*

CHAPTER 15

Made to Run

WHEN I WAS IN COLLEGE, I found myself desperate for a paycheck (as most college students are), so I applied to teach a kickboxing class at my local gym. Three nights a week I would lead an hour-long, cardio-packed session on kickboxing (at least that's what the brochure said). The humorous part of the story is that I was completely out of shape and knew *nothing* about kickboxing. The only knowledge I possessed on jabs and kicks was from a few Tae-Bo videos I had attempted in the privacy of my home. (If you are unfamiliar with the Tae-Bo craze of the late nineties, consider yourself lucky!) Much to my disbelief, I got the job. I had three weeks to prepare for class, so I set out on a mission to become fit.

Something you should know about me is that the moment I set my mind to do something, I go for it with all my heart. I become instantly passionate, even if it's about something as simple as folding the laundry. When I realized that three nights out of the week I would be solely responsible for the health and conditioning of a group of women, I set my sights on becoming a lean, mean kickboxing machine! As I stepped into the weight room on the first day, completely decked out in my workout clothes, I thought to myself, *Okay, I've got three weeks! This should be plenty of time to reach the peak of my physical fitness.*

Ha!

I spent hours in the gym that day, but I wasn't lifting weights or jogging on the treadmill. I spent my time going from one weight machine to another, reading the instructions on how to use them. I would awkwardly twist and distort my body just like the stick-figure man on the posted instructions was doing. I would finally get into a position to curl or lift, and with all the might in my out-of-shape body, I would grunt and gasp. My face would turn red and crinkle from straining to lift the weight set by the previous user.

After days of useless grunting and twisting, I was left with nothing but an aching, out-of-breath body. No physical-fitness achievements, no muscle burn, and definitely no *muscle*! I would then come home, turn on my workout videos, and pray I would glean some wisdom as I fumbled over each step. At the end of week one of preparation, I was ready to resign from my instructor position, and the class hadn't even started! I knew I needed help. Unfortunately, the gym didn't have any female fitness instructors, and I was leery of spending time alone with a male instructor. I would carefully watch the other instructors as they worked with their clients, moving to the machine closest to them in an attempt to overhear some of the tips they were offering.

Then one day, out of nowhere, a young man named John walked through the door to the weight room. He was alone and seemed a bit disoriented. He was quiet and kept to himself as I watched him go from machine to machine. He looked over each one intently, as if studying a textbook. He would fixate on one, adjust the weights a bit, and then, with the utmost attention to detail, perform the intended exercise to perfection. I stood in amazement. Who was this guy? I had never seen him in the gym before, yet he seemed to know everything about all the machines in the room.

Just one week away from the start date of my class, I was in the middle of attempting a bicep curl when John tapped my shoulder. "I'm sorry to bother you," he said, "but you're doing that wrong." In another situation I might have been offended or taken off guard by his bluntness, but not in this case! I *knew* I was doing it wrong, and I was so desperate to learn how to do it right. I spent the next three hours soaking up John's knowledge of fitness and nutrition.

It turns out that John was new to town, and the gym had recently hired him on as a fitness instructor. He didn't have any family or friends in town, so most of his days were spent learning about nutrition and fitness as he waited patiently for clients to enroll. For some reason the gym members weren't flocking to sign up for his instruction—maybe because he wasn't built like the typical macho fitness guys in our gym. But if you spent any time with John, you soon realized he was knowledgeable about the human body and how it works together for maximum results.

After receiving approval from my husband, I agreed to pay John for one week of training. The stipulation was that we would make no physical contact. He agreed, and we began to meet each day for two hours. As the week came to an end, I was finally beginning to feel a little more equipped to teach—and a little less out of breath!

On our last day of training, John had me jog on the treadmill for my usual ten-minute warm-up. He stood nearby looking at his schedule for the day like he always did. But on that day, something was different about him. As I sweated and gasped for breath, I noticed that John had something he wanted to say but was holding back. As I reached the end of my warm-up and regressed to a walk, I asked John, amid gulps of air, "Are you okay today?"

John had told me earlier in the week that he was an agnostic who geared his life around facts, not faith. Although I had taken a mental note of that, I continued making Christ a part of our daily conversations. I would simply talk about my relationship with God and what he was showing me through the fitness training. Most important, I never changed how I treated John. I showed him the same kindness after I learned of his disbelief in Christ as I had before I knew where he stood in his faith.

That last day of training, I could tell God was moving in John's heart. "You talk about God like he's someone you talk to on the phone every day," he said.

"Well, he *is* someone I talk to every day—just not on the phone," I told him.

I don't remember all the details of our conversation, but I do know that no training took place for those two hours. We sat right there in the gym lobby, with people rushing by, and I shared with John the love and grace of my Savior.

Several weeks later I had the privilege of escorting John to meet my pastor as John proclaimed his belief in the saving power of Christ in the presence of my entire church body. The beautiful part of this story has nothing to do with who I am or who John is, but who *Christ* is!

. . .

That crash course I had to prepare me for kickboxing class holds a number of applications for us as believers. Just as I embarked on the task of training in order to reach my goal of teaching the class, you are also in training. You may never have been a member of a gym or lifted a weight in your life. You may never have set foot on a treadmill or a racetrack, but you, child of God, are in the midst of a race. It is a race that has been "marked out" especially for you by the "perfecter of faith" (Hebrews 12:1-2, NIV). And along the way as you train for that race, you just may come upon fellow runners whom God has called you to encourage and speak truth to.

Something you should know about this race is that it requires training and endurance. It is filled with obstacles and flashy (but misleading) signs that read "Shortcut here!" But there's one thing that sets this race apart from other races—it has been run in advance. Jesus himself has run this race, and he has already reached the finish line.

Just as I looked to John as the standard of physical fitness, we must look to Christ as the standard of our *spiritual* fitness. The direction of your future comes down to one choice—will you stay in the race? Will you keep running? Will you fix your eyes on the finish line, or will you give in to your aching joints, your sore muscles, and the temptation to join those who are sipping water on the sidelines?

Precious one of the King, you were made to run! Here are some steps you need to take to run this race—and finish.

Wear Lightweight Clothing

When long-distance runners show up to race, what is their typical dress code? Do they wear bulky boots, layers of baggy clothes, and a loaded backpack? Not if they want to win! No, they wear lightweight clothing and shoes designed for speed and agility.

Hebrews 12:1 tells us to "throw off everything that hinders" (NIV). This mental picture makes it clear that an active step is required on our part. Sin needs to be taken seriously. We can't just limp along the racetrack, thinking our sin won't affect our Christian walk. We need to be proactive about getting rid of it so we can run the race well. And notice that it's not just sin we need to get rid of but everything that holds us back. That means not just the bad things but also the distractions—the good things that get in the way of the best things.

Before we go on, I encourage you to pause for a moment and reflect on a few questions:

What is weighing you down in your life right now?
Is there anything that is slowing you down from the race God has called you to?
What do you need to throw off, starting today?

Surround Yourself with Committed Runners

When you think of the people in your life you would consider your close friends, what attributes come to mind about each person? Do these friends love you despite your past, despite any future mistakes you might make, yet still encourage you to do the right thing? Or do these friends judge you and shame you for your sins? When you spend time with them, do you use up more breath gossiping about other people than you do encouraging one another to strengthen your relationship with Christ? Do these people go along with you in your moments of self-pity, or do they speak Scripture into your life, even when it's difficult to hear?

In order to run with complete perseverance, we must surround ourselves with people who are committed to the same goal and prize as we are. When we slow down, we need other people beside us who will help set the pace. And when we fall down, we need fellow runners who will reach down and help us up again.

It may be time to take a serious look at your "team" and see if there's anyone you may need to distance yourself from. I want you to be honest here. Do you have any friends who are holding you back from running the race God intended for you? The book of Proverbs has a number of warnings about the people we associate with closely. "The godly give good advice to their friends; the wicked lead them astray" (Proverbs 12:26). Do your friends give you good advice, or do they lead you astray?

> It's not just sin we need to get rid of but everything that holds us back. That means not just the bad things but also the distractions—the good things that get in the way of the best things.

I know it may seem harsh to pare down some of your teammates (and I am certainly not saying we shouldn't show grace and love to every one of God's children), but this is your future we're talking about! There is a big difference between the people you run into at the grocery store who deserve your kindness and the people you invite into your home for dinner on a regular basis. You must be wise in choosing your closest circle of friends. The people you currently run with may be weighing you down and hindering your race.

When I was a sophomore in college, I decided to become roommates with a girl I barely knew. We worked together at the same place and were both desperate to be free of our parents, so we jumped into sharing a duplex together before learning much about one another. It quickly became apparent that we were two very different people. Namely, I was a Christian and she was not. I thought I was strong enough to be able to influence her to change and not the other way around, but that's not the way things worked out.

My roommate was into sex, drugs, and more sex and drugs. And although she was respectful enough of my standards not to bring either one into our duplex, I realized after a few months of living together that her constant conversations about those topics were desensitizing me. Before long I noticed that I was letting curse words slip from my mouth here and there and allowing my midriff to show when I had never done so before. As more time went by, I even found myself justifying her actions more and more in my head: "Oh, that's not so bad. She just doesn't know any better."

I knew I was in trouble when one night she brought her sinful lifestyle into our place. Evidently she could sense that my standards had dropped low enough for her to get away with it. That moment was a turning point for me—a wake-up call that I couldn't afford to keep putting myself in a position to compromise what I stood for.

We are foolish when we believe we are strong enough to withstand a continuous sinful influence in our lives—or, for that matter, a continuous *complacent* influence in our lives. We may have friends who are not actively engaging in sinful activities, but neither are they actively living out their faith. These believers stagnate because they huddle together with other complacent believers who have brainwashed one another to believe it's okay to remain safely within the walls of the church, never venturing into the unknown territory of following God's leading. In my opinion, that kind of contagious apathy can be just as deadly to our faith as blatant sin.

Drop Any Unhealthy Addictions

If you're familiar with any athletes who are serious about their sport, you know they are equally serious about everything that goes into their bodies. They watch their carb intake and their caffeine consumption, and they stay away from vices, like cigarettes or alcohol, that could impair their performance. The same goes for us as Christians. If we're going to build up the endurance we need to make it to the finish line, we must clean out our lives from top to bottom.

Sometimes we don't know (or refuse to acknowledge) what's best for us, so we must be humble and vulnerable enough to accept the advice of our trainer. Maybe after years of practice, you've gotten used to toting around your unhealthy baggage. Maybe you've even managed to hide it from other people. But you cannot hide it from God. He desires your full attention and devotion, and he sees every dark corner of your life that the human eye cannot. "The LORD sees every heart and knows every plan and thought" (1 Chronicles 28:9).

> There are so many things in our lives that are not bad in themselves, but they become dangerous when we make them into idols or when they start controlling us.

There are so many things in our lives that are not bad in themselves, but they become dangerous when we make them into idols or when they start controlling us. The things we put in our bodies, the things we plant in our minds, the things we obsess over—any of those have the potential to become addictions. Please understand that I am of the opinion that the Lord desires this life to be a blessing to his creations! I believe the Creator of the universe breathed life into us not only for his delight but for our delight as well. I'm not saying a weekly trip to McDonald's is a sin. I don't believe a glass of wine at Christmas dinner is harmful. Surfing the web from time to time, keeping a neat and tidy home, exercising on a regular basis—all those can be good and glorifying things if they're kept within their proper context, with the intention of bringing honor to God.

In order to recognize where you have blurred the line between enjoying a particular element of life and being dependent on it, I encourage you to ask yourself the following questions:

Question 1: Do I engage in this behavior without conscious thought of it?

Question 2: Have I become too comfortable with this practice? In other words, do I no longer feel awkward or guilty while involved in this behavior even though I probably should?

Question 3: Do I naturally respond with this practice when presented with a stressful or negative situation?

Question 4: Does the thought of giving up this behavior provoke anxiety or seem impossible to do?

Question 5: Do I have people close to me expressing words of concern or caution in regard to this particular behavior?

We will one day gain the treasure and reward of eternal life. But while we are here, in these temporary dwellings, we must run the race with perseverance. By God's grace, we can join Paul in saying, "I press on to reach the end of the race and receive the heavenly prize for which God, through Christ Jesus, is calling us" (Philippians 3:14).

> YOU ARE NAMED BY GOD: *You are a victor.*

CHAPTER 16

Gifted to Serve

WHEN I WAS IN HIGH SCHOOL, my home church desperately needed nursery workers to take care of children during weeknight activities. At that time in my life, I felt I had much better things to spend my time on (such as boys) than watching a bunch of screaming, snot-nosed toddlers run around and pull each other's hair. Much to my dismay, my grandmother signed me up to help (she obviously felt I didn't have anything better to do). Every week I would grudgingly shuffle my selfish teenage feet into the church nursery. I would sulk and complain the entire two hours, doing as little child care as possible until the parents came, and then I would dart out of the building with the greatest of speed.

Regardless of my age, I knew better. Each week in that nursery, I would feel subtle twinges of guilt running through my bones as I griped and complained. Even as a teenager, I knew the Lord had called me to serve—and to do it with the attitude of serving him, not people.

No matter how old we are, it's part of the Christian life to respond to the unexplainable urge to serve. As we mature in our faith, so does our focus about how we can best use our gifts for the glory of God. Because each one of us is made purposefully by God, he doesn't waste any part of us. From our birth, he has been developing the gifts, abilities, personalities, and talents he has woven into us so they can be used for his purposes.

> In your relationships with one another, have the same mindset
> as Christ Jesus:
> Who, being in very nature God, did not consider equality
> with God something to be used to his own advantage; rather,
> he made himself nothing by taking the very nature of a servant,
> being made in human likeness. PHILIPPIANS 2:5-7 (NIV)

Once we become followers of Christ, our lives are no longer our own. We are called to "offer [our] bodies as a living sacrifice" (Romans 12:1, NIV). This means that our lives should be daily offerings to Christ on the altar of service. When we are able to grasp this truth, serving takes on added meaning and purpose. It may be strange to think about it this way, but we were created to serve God through serving *others*. Allow that to sink in a bit. We were created by God and then received his salvation so that we might be God's hands and feet in this world. Serving is putting aside our fleshly desires and placing God and others before ourselves.

When people think of serving, they almost always think of it as a physical action—perhaps like charity work. That's part of it, but serving isn't just something we do; it's something we *are*. Jesus had an attitude—an entire lifestyle—of service that he calls us to imitate. Jesus did not stutter or stammer in his call for his children to serve. It is not an option; it's a commandment. Our acts of service should not simply be done if we have spare time or because our grandmothers made us do it. If our future is going to be the reflection of the Messiah, we must serve as he did—that is, making service a way of life.

> Because each one of us is made purposefully by God, he doesn't waste any part of us.

When Jesus came to this earth, he had every right to come to demonstrate his authority as master over us and over all of creation. But instead, he came as a humble servant. He didn't arrive in this world asking, "What can people do for me?" but rather, "What can I do for people?" Christ set the ultimate example of servanthood, and we are to model our lives after his.

Let me fill you in on an important truth about serving others—in God's eyes, there are no "little" acts or "big" acts. As long as you are being obedient to God and working completely for him and for no one else, it doesn't matter if you find yourself in the restroom scrubbing toilets or in front of the church leading worship. Your sacrifice to the Lord is equally as sweet.

What are *you* doing to serve the body of believers? Do you help with child care? Do you send out get-well cards to people in the congregation? Do you sweep the floors after a meal? Do you count the money from the offering plate? Do you organize the food pantry? Do you take pictures when new members join? Do you pray for the church staff and its members? All of these are beautiful acts of service to our Lord if they are offered to him as pure and genuine sacrifices (and yes, that means no complaining!).

If you are having a difficult time thinking of something you do to serve, what do you think is holding you back from accepting God's call?

It's important that we get this right, because when we reach the doorway to eternity, we will all give an account to God of what we did and did not do with our lives and what we have been given. "'As surely as I live,' says the Lord, 'every knee will bow before me; every tongue will acknowledge God.' So then, each of us will give an account of ourselves to God" (Romans 14:11-12, NIV).

Our days on earth will be filled with giving our time and energy to something—a career, a hobby, a home, a sport, money. Yet which of these things has eternal significance? One day, as we stand in the presence of our Creator, all our excuses, all our justifications, all our procrastination and laziness will have no place in the courtyard of Christ. It is only when we choose complete service to God that our lives—and our futures—take on eternal value.

God-Given Gifts

I am so excited to dig into this part of the book with you because I personally know the joy that consumes our lives when we set our hearts on serving the Lord with the abilities he has hardwired into our being.

This is a time for you to reflect on your unique, God-given abilities—in other words, your spiritual gifts! For some of you, this may be a refresher course. Maybe you've spent time exploring and uncovering your spiritual gifts and are currently using those gifts in full devotion to the Lord. For others, it's quite possible you've never pinpointed your gifts, or maybe you thought God gave things like that to other people, not you. If this is you, let me hold my palms to your precious face and tell you, "Created child of God, of course you have a spiritual gift to use for his glory!" (see Ephesians 2:10; 1 Corinthians 12:7).

So if every believer has a spiritual gift, why are our churches desperate for volunteers? Why do so many people show up for service but do nothing more than warm a seat? I believe if all the members involved in a church body devoted themselves to using their spiritual gifts, church buildings wouldn't be able to house all the people who wanted to attend. And it would be difficult to find an unsaved soul within a thirty-mile radius of the building!

It is only when we choose complete service to God that our lives—and our futures—take on eternal value.

From my perspective, there are two reasons why Christians don't effectively use their God-given abilities (and I have personally fallen into both categories at some point in my life). First, some believers don't know what their spiritual gift is. Maybe someone has nudged them in a certain direction before, but they've never pinpointed their precise ability. Second, some believers are under the false impression that they aren't good enough to use their gift for the Lord—or that if they attempted to use it, they would be rejected by other people.

As we begin this conversation about spiritual gifts, it's important to cover some groundwork on a few basic questions:

Where do spiritual gifts come from?
Whom are they given to?
Why are they given?

Here's what Scripture has to say about spiritual gifts:

There are different kinds of spiritual gifts, but the same Spirit is the source of them all. There are different kinds of service, but we serve the same Lord. God works in different ways, but it is the same God who does the work in all of us.

A spiritual gift is given to each of us so we can help each other. To one person the Spirit gives the ability to give wise advice; to another the same Spirit gives a message of special knowledge. The same Spirit gives great faith to another, and to someone else the one Spirit gives the gift of healing.

He gives one person the power to perform miracles, and another the ability to prophesy. He gives someone else the ability to discern whether a message is from the Spirit of God or from another spirit. Still another person is given the ability to speak in unknown languages, while another is given the ability to interpret what is being said. It is the one and only Spirit who distributes all these gifts. He alone decides which gift each person should have. I CORINTHIANS 12:4-11

Our spiritual gifts are not just skills and talents we've worked on or picked up along the way. They're given directly from the Holy Spirit. These gifts are to be highly treasured, for ultimately they represent the Lord's work in us and through us (see 1 Corinthians 12:4-6).

If you are a believer in Christ, you have the absolute privilege of possessing a beautiful spiritual gift from God. You may have yet to unwrap it and use it, but God has given you the ability to do so. It is a privilege we enjoy as living reflections of God's light in a dark world.

We are given spiritual gifts for two reasons: to glorify God and to build up the church body. Paul says, "God has put the body together, giving greater honor to the parts that lacked it, so that there should be no division in the body, but that its parts should have equal concern for each other" (1 Corinthians 12:24-25, NIV). Nowhere in Scripture are we told that we are given gifts to bring glory to ourselves, to meet a personal need, or to make ourselves feel better. These gifts are always used for the greater good of the body of Christ. In other words, church is not a spectator sport! We have been given gifts, and God expects us to use them.

You might think you have nothing to offer the body of believers. You might have bought the lie that because of who you were in your past, you are permanently marked as useless. Or you might think you are doing no harm to the church by sitting there for worship and then heading to the parking lot as quickly as possible after the final song. You might even be patting yourself on the back, thinking, *Well, at least I go to church! My buddies at work don't even go.*

I'm sorry to get in your face a bit here, but sometimes there's no soft way to say it: if you're a believer in Christ and your time involved in your church body can be clocked from the moment you take a seat at the beginning of worship until the moment you snap the seatbelt around your waist as you leave, you are not only completely missing out on the blessing God desires to give you, but you are failing as a part of your church. You are a "suffering part." And when "one part suffers, every part suffers with it" (1 Corinthians 12:26, NIV).

With that background covered, let's make this personal. What is *your* spiritual gift? First, get a Bible and take a look at the gifts listed for us in Scripture (1 Corinthians 12:1-11; 1 Corinthians 12:27-28; Ephesians 4:11; Romans 12:6-8).

Administration	Knowledge
Apostleship	Leadership
Discernment	Mercy
Evangelism	Miracles
Exhortation	Pastoring
Faith	Prophecy
Giving	Service
Healing	Teaching
Helping	Tongues
Interpretation	Wisdom

Did you have any idea there were so many different gifts laid out in Scripture? And get this—these lists aren't exhaustive. They are intended to serve as general categories rather than a complete checklist.

Whatever your gift, the most important thing is that you use it in a way that honors the Lord. And let me tell you, when you start actively using your spiritual gift, something crazy happens—God shows up!

Don't Forget to Breathe

Imagine that you're in the midst of a rigorous exercise regimen. Your trainer has instructed you to jog five miles on the treadmill. As you painfully take step after step, trying to make it through that last agonizing mile, the trainer leans over your shoulder and whispers in your ear, "Hey, don't forget to breathe." That's kind of what it's like when we fail to use the spiritual gifts we've been given.

The Bible warns us, "Do not quench the Spirit" (1 Thessalonians 5:19, NIV). When we disregard our spiritual gifts and don't allow them a place in our lives, we are actually smothering the movement of the Holy Spirit's fire inside of us. And that has an impact not only on our own lives but within our church body as well. But, loved one, let me share a beautiful truth with you. If you choose to give energy and attention to your God-given abilities, this will soon become like breathing for you. Using your gifts for the Lord will become so natural, so consuming, and so much a part of who you are that you won't be able to help doing it! It will become your spiritual breathing.

> God, the giver of all gifts, knew exactly what he was doing when he created you. He designed you specially to fill a role that no one but you can fulfill.

As we start learning together how to breathe, I want to remind you of one thing: God, the giver of all gifts, knew exactly what he was doing when he created you. When it comes to spiritual gifts, he didn't make a mistake or skip over you. He designed you specially to fill a role that no one but you can fulfill. And whatever it is that God calls you to do, he'll equip you and give you exactly what you need to do it.

My desire is that you will leave this chapter with all the confidence you need to start (or continue) pursuing your gift. In order to get there, we'll need to take a little time to do some self-evaluation.

Question 1: What are you passionate about?

Start by simply asking yourself, *What do I love to do?* What task, project, or role do you want to perform? What energizes you and makes your heart beat with anticipation? Our passions and our gifts go together—if God gives us a particular gift, he also gives us the desire to pursue it.

A word of warning when dealing with your passions, though: don't allow your emotions to carry you away. Emotions can be deceiving and can therefore taint the true desires God has placed in your heart. As long as your "want to" has everything to do with serving God and others, you are in the clear. But if your desire has anything to do with meeting your personal needs, it's probably time to reexamine your motives.

For example, in James 3:1 we are told that not everyone should pursue the role of teacher. If you long to be in a position of authority because of the honor associated with the title or because it gives you a platform to have your voice heard, it is most likely not a God-given desire (see Galatians 6:4; Romans 9:20-21).

Question 2: What are you good at?

It's uncomfortable for many of us to talk about the things we're good at because we don't want to feel like we're boasting about ourselves. But for just a few moments we're going to lay those fears aside and take an honest inventory of what God has given us. After all, we're not really boasting about ourselves but about the Creator who made us. We'll claim 1 Corinthians 1:31: "Let the one who boasts boast in the Lord" (NIV).

As you consider the areas in your life in which you have been successful, it might help to ask yourself this question: "What are areas of giftedness in my life that other people have confirmed?" For example, my church family is blessed with a gifted, God-honoring worship leader. It is easy for anyone in the congregation to see that he has God-given abilities in music and leadership. My husband and I make it a point to tell him on a regular basis what a blessing his ministry is to our church and to us—to confirm those gifts to him.

On the other hand, if you feel you are a gifted leader but no one seems to be following, you might be serving in the wrong area. If you attempt to serve in a particular ministry and it just doesn't work out, take heart in knowing that, without a doubt, you *do* have a gift instilled by God. It is just a matter of finding it!

The only way to discover your gifts is by getting involved in what God is doing. So don't be afraid to try new things. If it's not a good fit, don't look at it as a defeat; just consider it additional information in your assessment of yourself. As I always say when I crash and burn at an attempt to serve God, "Now I'm just smarter than I used to be!"

Question 3: Where do you see a need?

The final step in determining how to use your gifts is to take a look around your church and your community. Where are the open doors? Where are the needs? One easy place to begin is to pay special attention to the announcements during your worship service or to take note of your church bulletin or newsletter. Is your pastor continually asking for nursery volunteers? Are the leaders asking for prayer about a specific need? Is there a family in your church that is suffering financially? An interesting thing about spiritual gifts is that we may not even know we have them until we are busy meeting a need and in the process discover an area of gifting.

Fairly early in my life I knew I had a desire to teach. I agreed to lead a women's small group because I knew there was a need, and it was only after accepting the position that I realized I possessed such a gift. Plainly put, you don't know what you are good at until you try!

If right now you find yourself in the position of wanting to use your gifts but not knowing where to begin, I'd like to encourage you to see the needs around you and ponder how you might be able to meet one of them. This is, after all, what God has called each of us to do: "Whenever we have the opportunity, we should do good to everyone—especially to those in the family of faith" (Galatians 6:10).

A Note to Those Who Have Fallen

Maybe as you've read this chapter you've been thinking to yourself, *That's nice, but it doesn't apply to me.* Perhaps you have fallen so deep and so far away from God that you're convinced he will never be able to use you or your gifts. If that's you, loved one, let this encouragement from Scripture fall fresh on your battered and bruised heart as it did on mine over the course of my transformation.

But first, let me give a little background about this story. The Israelites have been whining for a king to lead them, even though God tells them he alone is their king and they don't need a human king like the surrounding nations. But they beg and beg until he gives in and lets them have what they want.

In 1 Samuel 12 we come upon a scene in which the Israelites are celebrating with their new king, Saul. In turning from the rule of the Lord to the rule of a mere man, the Israelites have lost something great. However, even though the people sinned by disbelieving the Lord would take care of them, they are encouraged to keep pressing on. When they come to God in repentance, he gives them a second chance. Through the judge Samuel they receive this message: "You have certainly done wrong, but make sure now that you worship the LORD with all your heart, and don't turn your back on him" (1 Samuel 12:20).

Yes, they disobeyed. But this comes as no surprise to the Lord, as it is no shock to him when you or I sin. God takes sin seriously, but he is always ready to take back those with humble hearts. Just as he told the Israelites, he is telling us today, "The LORD will not abandon his people, because that would dishonor his great name. For it has pleased the LORD to make you his very own people" (verse 22).

If (and that's a big if) fallen children of God are broken and repentant—in other words, if they take no part in their past sin and have turned away from it completely—I believe the church body has no place to refuse the sincere and wholehearted service of those fallen servants. The purpose of church leadership is to encourage and build fully restored servants of Christ. To deny repentant sinners access to church ministry would be denying that the blood of Jesus Christ is enough to cover all sins. Besides, if the church body were to refuse people the right to serve based on their past sins, churches across the world would be empty! (see 1 Samuel 12:20-22).

Of course we should be wise as a church, and we are charged to carefully call out sin within the body. However, our goal should be the restoration of the fellow brother or sister in Christ, not judgment. Scripture tells us, "Speak and act as those who are going to be judged by the law that gives freedom, because judgment without mercy will be shown to anyone who has not been merciful. Mercy triumphs over judgment" (James 2:12-13, NIV).

Wherever you are on your journey toward pursuing your gifts, I pray you will remember this: you are always serving for an audience of one. If your service is being done to the glory of God, it makes no difference who criticizes you or questions you or judges you. Keep pressing on for the Lord. Remember, your King only has eyes for you. Out of your love for him, don't let your eyes wander.

YOU ARE NAMED BY GOD: *You are divinely gifted.*

CHAPTER 17

Keep Your Eyes
on the Prize

LIFE IS FULL OF DISTRACTIONS AND DELUSIONS. Something as simple as the routines of our daily schedules can lull us into missing our God-given purpose. Even the familiarity of "going through the motions" can seduce us into spiritual complacency, which if left unchecked will inevitably suffocate our potential and cause us to miss all that God has for us.

When I was in the first year of my graduate program in counseling, I often found myself getting distracted by the mundane paperwork. The days seemed relentless as I read textbooks, took tests, wrote papers, read more books, and took more tests. I would spend all day in class and wind up completely exhausted by the end of the day. I felt guilty that I was not at home cleaning or cooking or learning some new "wife" skill. I started doubting my inner calling to be an advocate of change on behalf of others. So many days I just wanted to give up. I wondered if anyone would ever hire me, if I really had what it took to help anybody.

But each time I fell into a slump I would remember the year to come—my internship. In the second year of the program I would be given the opportunity to actually begin counseling people. This was what I was waiting for! The only way I could get through the grind of papers, reading assignments, and tests was to keep focused on the prize—my first real, live counseling session with a real, live person.

When year two of grad school arrived, I got my first counseling assignment and discovered to my surprise that I'd been thrown into the deep end. My job would be to work for a hospice, doing grief counseling with a young woman who had lost her mother a few months earlier. I was terrified as I prepared to meet with her (although, ironically, I found out later that she was just as terrified to meet with me).

But during those weekly, hour-long visits, something beautiful happened. Mostly I just listened and asked this woman to elaborate on specific areas of her grief. The process of sharing in the life and pain of another person captivated me even more each time we met. It was a rare privilege to be let into that private world of someone else's suffering. Suddenly all the coursework was worth it. And to think there were moments I had considered giving it up!

In our walk of faith, we often need to spend time studying up in God's school before he sends us out to a certain assignment or calling. It's in those times especially that we need to keep our eyes on the prize. We can't give up now, before we've reached the finish line. We need Paul's perspective: "I consider my life worth nothing to me; my only aim is to finish the race and complete the task the Lord Jesus has given me—the task of testifying to the good news of God's grace" (Acts 20:24, NIV).

Let's face it: everyday life can get us down. Some days it feels like we're just going through the motions, doing all the things we did the day before—the same morning routine, the same news show, the same route to work, the same responsibilities at home, the same bedtime rituals—and then we lie down in the same bed, only to start all over again the next day. No wonder people throughout the world are asking, "What is my purpose in life?"

Our society feeds us the lie that life is boring and meaningless unless it's constantly filled with fun, success, money, and recognition. Almost subconsciously, we focus on what we are getting out of life rather than what we are putting into it.

> Something as simple as the routines of our daily schedules can lull us into missing our God-given purpose.

If you are feeling bored or bogged down by monotony, take some time to ask God to grant you a sense of revival. Sweet child of God, no one in this world can love you the way your Father does. He has a future in store for you that is more thrilling than anything you can imagine. People may limit you. Your own flesh may limit you. But with the omnipotent King on your team, the sky—the heavenly sky—is the limit.

And that future is not some elusive mystery, far off in the distance. The plans God has for you are something you can know now—and start embracing now. For starters, we can embrace the truth that God has sent each of us into the world as his ambassadors. This was part of Jesus' prayer for his followers (that includes you!): "As you sent me into the world, I have sent them into the world" (John 17:18, NIV). Just as Jesus came to shine his light into the lives of others, he has also sent us out to do the same. This is where our great reward lies.

This reward God promises is not about us—it's nothing for us to boast about, and it's not for our personal gain. This reward is also not something we will fully grasp in this lifetime. God alone knows the unimaginable joy and reward that await those of us who take up the call to be bold bearers of his name. As citizens of heaven but residents on this earth, we should never get discouraged, because we live in a constant state of victory. Our great reward is not only that the blood of Christ has been spilled on our behalf but also that we look forward to the day of his return (see 1 Thessalonians 4:16-17).

> People may limit you. Your own flesh may limit you. But with the omnipotent King on your team, the sky—the heavenly sky—is the limit.

This doesn't mean that we ignore or neglect our responsibilities or that we let our lives on this earth pass us by. It means we live each day with an eye to what Christ will do in the future. If we keep our focus moment by moment on the promised reward of an eternity spent with him, we will be living for the things that truly matter.

As we look at the life Jesus Christ lived when he walked this earth, it's obvious that he knew beyond the shadow of a doubt what God had called him to do. How could Jesus be so clear about his assignment, so committed to keeping his eyes fixed on the goal? It was because he was intimately connected to his Father and maintained direct communication with him at all times. Jesus put it this way: "I don't speak on my own authority. The Father who sent me has commanded me what to say and how to say it. And I know his commands lead to eternal life; so I say whatever the Father tells me to say" (John 12:49-50).

Jesus understood precisely what his purpose was each moment on earth, and he also knew when his mission was complete. Even in his death—his final act of submission to God in a human body—Jesus remained faithful to God's plan for him. From the cross Jesus shouted, "'Father, I entrust my spirit into your hands!' And with those words he breathed his last" (Luke 23:46).

This assignment might seem as final as it can get, but that's not the end of the story. His last breath may have marked the completion of his human mission on earth, but it was only the beginning of *our* mission. We have been given the responsibility and privilege of continuing Christ's purpose until the day of his return. Jesus made his assignment clear to us with these words, otherwise known as the great commission: "Go and make disciples of all the nations, baptizing them in the name of the Father and the Son and the Holy Spirit. Teach these new disciples to obey all the commands I have given you" (Matthew 28:19-20).

There are two important characteristics to note about this assignment. First, it isn't just given to the "spiritual elite." The call to take the name of Jesus into every corner of the world is not intended only for pastors and missionaries and Bible teachers but for every believer. Second, the great commission is not a great *suggestion*. It isn't an option or a possibility; it is a mandatory command in the life of every Christ follower.

Whether you realize it or not, you have a life-changing message to share with other people. Your life may seem boring, routine, and uneventful. You like the idea of people's lives being changed for Christ, but you certainly don't see how you could have anything to do with it. Oh, but wait right there, child of God. God has given you a beautiful story to tell. Your *life* is your story! It is a precious book filled with page upon page of hard times, good times, times of doubt, times of celebration—and God's redemptive work in the midst of it all. This is not just any message—it is a handwritten account penned by the loving hand of God.

Getting in the Game

It's one thing to know God has an assignment for our future. But when it comes to the daily realities of life, there are many obstacles that hinder us from living a life of radical faith (in other words, a life of purpose, joy, peace, boldness, and hope). Even after we have experienced the sacrificial healing of our past and the transformation of our present, we may still get stuck sometimes.

I found myself stumped by this problem. Why is it, even though we know deep in our souls that we have been named by God, that we continue to give in to that addiction? Why do we find ourselves right back in the same group of ungodly friends, going to the same ungodly places? Why do we turn the television to that same old reality show that we know will fill our minds with unwholesome images? Why do we get right back in the habit of skipping church? Why do we continue making excuses about why we aren't good enough to serve in a specific ministry? Why do we let that lost soul pass us by in the grocery store when we feel the Spirit compelling us to speak to her about Christ? Why can't we just dare to live every day for Christ . . . every day as if it were our last?

I knew I wasn't alone in this quest, so I decided to seek help in getting answers. I asked all kinds of people from different walks of life one simple question: "What is the one thing that hinders you from living each day as a bold believer who is sold out for Christ?"

The answers varied in some of the specifics. Some people said, "There are just too many distractions in this life" or "I don't have enough time and energy" or "My fears hold me back" or "I keep trying and failing" or "I don't want people to think I'm a freak." But the underlying theme was resoundingly the same across the board: it's a daily struggle to let Sunday filter over into Monday, Tuesday, Wednesday, Thursday, Friday, and Saturday . . . in order to get back to Sunday again!

> Stagnation doesn't happen overnight—it's the result of a subtle, gradual decline.

You see, it's not that we as believers don't possess the *desire* to live boldly. Most of the people I talked to are devoted followers of Christ. The majority of them attend church on a regular basis, serve in a ministry, lead moral lives, and seek to live as bright lights in a dark world. None of us intend to become complacent in our walks with the Lord. I know from personal experience that stagnation doesn't happen overnight—it's the result of a subtle, gradual decline that affects us all at some point. Yes, even the most righteous Christ followers can unknowingly succumb to the clutches of mundane living.

That process plays out internally something like this:

Oh, I will talk to her about Jesus tomorrow. Now just doesn't seem like a convenient time.

Oh yeah, I should invite him to church. Maybe next week. . . .

You know, I have really been meaning to get involved at church. I just don't have time right now.

I know that family is in need, but things are just really tight for us right now.

I'll quit tomorrow. . . .

I'll start tomorrow. . . .

Before we realize it, days and weeks have ticked by with our excuses, and there we are, still sitting on the sidelines. It's time to get in the game!

If you're feeling at a loss about how to get off the bench, take heart! God has not left us alone in this. "The Advocate, the Holy Spirit, whom the Father will send in my name, will teach you all things and will remind you of everything I have said to you" (John 14:26, NIV). When you become a Christian, you are instantly given the gift of the Holy Spirit. That filling is immediate and permanent. But we need to be intentional about keeping that relationship a vibrant part of our lives. This is important, because the use—or misuse—of the Holy Spirit is what separates the stagnant believer from the bold believer.

We cannot expect to experience daily renewal unless the Holy Spirit is at work in us. It is not enough to go to church; it is not enough to live a moral life; it is not enough to make wise decisions; it is not enough to read the Bible regularly. If we want to be radical for Christ, we need the Holy Spirit to divinely rock our world. Pray for the refreshing water of the Holy Spirit to fill your life—not just once when you come to faith, not once a week at church, but every day.

I started experiencing this daily adventure with the Lord once I began surrendering my stuff to him every morning—my thoughts, my desires, my needs, my plans, my feelings, my self-doubts, and my questions. Like any new habit, the daily routine of asking to be filled with the Holy Spirit didn't happen immediately. At first it felt downright scary and difficult, and definitely unnatural. In fact, for days and even weeks into this, I didn't feel like doing it at all. But the more I did it, the more natural it became. And the more natural it became, the more a part of my identity it became, until it gradually felt more and more like breathing.

The same can be true for you. You don't have to wonder if you qualify for the Holy Spirit—the Lord himself guarantees the arrival of his Spirit. All you have to do is invite him in. "You . . . have also heard the truth, the Good News that God saves you. And when you believed in Christ, he identified you as his own by giving you the Holy Spirit, whom he promised long ago. The Spirit is God's guarantee that he will give us the inheritance he promised and that he has purchased us to be his own people" (Ephesians 1:13-14).

• • •

Today is the opportunity to embrace your mission—your future! No more looking on from the sidelines, watching the pastor or Bible study leader, wishing you could be more like him or her. Now is the time! And the first step in doing so is to make a daily commitment to start each morning with a filling of the Holy Spirit from the tips of your toes to the top of your head.

Instead of complaining that your life is in a rut or you just don't "feel God" anymore, why don't you give full-blown surrender to the Holy Spirit a try? Ask him to help you keep your eyes fixed on God—the true prize. He is the only one who can completely renew you—and the way you look at the world.

YOU ARE NAMED BY GOD: *You are his ambassador.*

CHAPTER 18

Radically Reformed

I ALMOST DIED THE OTHER DAY in an attempt to live radically for my God.

Well, okay. That might be a teensy bit dramatic, but it got your attention, right? I had no idea when I woke up that morning that God would give me a personal glimpse into what it can cost to live a life of extreme Christianity.

On that summer day my church initiated a community outreach event. Several of us gathered in a parking lot in a busy area of town. We proudly displayed our new church T-shirts as we set out on a mission to serve free hot dogs and bottled water to our community between 11 a.m. and 2 p.m. There was no catch. There was no church sales pitch. There wasn't even a donation bucket. It was just a simple act of kindness from our church body to our community. Our one desire was to show our neighbors a small portion of our Savior's love and generosity by providing them with a free lunch and a bottle of water on a scorching East Texas day.

As we gathered under our canopy and prepared for a fast-paced day of serving hot dogs, we were confident the thousand buns, weenies, and bottles we'd prepared would disappear within the first hour. Who would pass up a free lunch?

As the hot sun bore down and the hours passed by, we soon realized our day was not going according to plan. No one seemed to be stopping. Sure, there were a few cars here and there, but we had a thousand hot dogs and a thousand bottles we needed to move!

So we decided to make a few more signs. Maybe with better advertising people would begin pouring in. We drafted messages on a few more pieces of poster board, making sure to bold the word *free*. The people in our group began spreading out, waving the signs along the busy street and motioning for the cars to turn into the parking lot. And still we had gone through a grand total of just fifty hot dogs.

From their cars, people would signal their hands to us in dismissal, mouth the words "No, thank you" through the window, and turn their heads to avoid eye contact. Even when we emphasized that this wouldn't cost them anything, they would laugh and say, "Nothing is free" or "What's the catch?" People couldn't understand why we would give them something free of charge. And because they couldn't understand it, they wanted nothing to do with it.

And then came the turning point in the day. One minute one of my fellow church members was standing by my side, and the next minute he was gone! I panned the grassy knoll where the rest of us were perched, but there was no sign of him. Then I glanced toward the road and spotted him in the middle of the turn lane, cars flying past him. As I watched, he reached into a car and handed out bottles for an entire family. Before I had a chance to pick up my jaw from the ground, my friend came jogging back with a huge smile on his face. "Hey!" he said. "That was fun!"

And from that moment on, we were crazy people for Christ. Each time the light turned red and the cars came to a complete stop, we would scatter through the stopped traffic yelling, "Free water!" We would hold the bottles right in front of the cars until the drivers rolled down their windows to take them from us. We got a wide range of reactions to our offer. Some people were confused but grateful. Others told us we were crazy. We even had a group of young men repeatedly pass by shouting obscenities at us. And then there was the near-death part of the experience, which came when the light turned green and I was still in the street. Oops.

I know my little adventure was nothing compared to the experience of Christians in other countries who suffer and are even martyred for their faith. But that afternoon did give me a new perspective on what it means to live on the edge for my God. Now, I'm not encouraging everyone to run into the street and chance sudden death for the sake of Christ. I am, however, urging you to be bold about your faith. Don't be afraid to catch people off guard and force them to see the love and kindness of the God you serve.

It's true that we got some strange looks that day, but we also had the couple who looked at the church logo on the bottled water and said, "You know what? We're new to the area and looking for a church home. We should come try you guys out." We saw the astonished smiles on people's faces when we said, "There's no catch. We're just doing this because we love you!" Those small victories keep me pressing on in my quest to live radically for Christ.

Living as a Radical

Our society gets a little nervous about the word *radical*. The concept tends to conjure up images of thrill seekers, adrenaline junkies, freaks, or even religious extremists. But in my book (and this *is* my book, after all), I see being radical as purposely living outside the box of religion and culture. You see, in order for you and me to do extraordinary things in the name of Jesus, we must also claim a measure of reckless passion for our Savior.

I believe God wants us to be visionaries and change makers in our world—people who pioneer new ways of thinking and behaving as we draw others to him. God has wired us to live on the edge—to be driven to know him more deeply and to be addicted to bringing people to him. It's important to point out that we can't attempt to live radically on our own, though. Radical living without God can only result in addiction or slavery to sin.

There's one woman in particular who struggled with being radical on her own terms, apart from God. The first half of her life she was mastered by her sinful nature, her flesh. She was driven by her insecurities and the negative opinions of others, and she was addicted to the Band-Aid fix of unhealthy relationships. That is, until the day she met another radical who taught her a new way and showed her how to focus her drive in the right direction. We meet this woman at a well in Samaria two thousand years ago. Let's jump into her story, shall we?

> "Please, sir," the woman said, "give me this water! Then I'll never be thirsty again, and I won't have to come here to get water."
>
> "Go and get your husband," Jesus told her.

"I don't have a husband," the woman replied.

Jesus said, "You're right! You don't have a husband—
for you have had five husbands, and you aren't even married
to the man you're living with now. You certainly spoke
the truth!" JOHN 4:15-18

Now watch what happens when one radical looks into the heart
of another radical:

The woman said, "I know the Messiah is coming—the
one who is called Christ. When he comes, he will explain
everything to us."

Then Jesus told her, "I AM the Messiah!"

Just then his disciples came back. They were shocked to find
him talking to a woman, but none of them had the nerve to ask,
"What do you want with her?" or "Why are you talking to her?"
The woman left her water jar beside the well and ran back to
the village, telling everyone, "Come and see a man who told me
everything I ever did! Could he possibly be the Messiah?" So the
people came streaming from the village to see him.

JOHN 4:25-30

I want to point out here that the mere fact that Jesus is taking
time to speak to and interact with this woman indicates that he
is a radical, for he is surely breaking the traditions and norms of
his culture. The woman is a Samaritan, a mixed race of Jew and
Gentile that was rejected altogether by the Jews of that time. In
that day, it would have been considered improper for a man like
Jesus to speak to a woman in public at all.

And if there's any question about Jesus being a radical, his bold honesty leaves no doubt. Jesus does not beat around the bush or sugarcoat his sales pitch to win the woman over. He lovingly points out her sin, corrects her misunderstandings about God, and tells her how to receive eternal life.

Then the woman responds to Jesus' truth in a radical move on her part. She immediately goes home and tells everyone she knows about the Messiah.

That part of the story amazes me. This woman could have kept her conversion to herself and thought about it for several days before telling anyone else. She could have been scared to death to go back to the one place where everyone knew her reputation and just kept quiet about the whole thing. She could have downplayed her part in the story and simply said, "Come see this man at the well" instead of confessing *her* story, *her* sin. She could have assumed that God would clean up her past before he could use her as his witness. But no, she allows God to turn her mistakes into his miracle, and in turn, many people experience truth that day.

> In order for you and me to do extraordinary things in the name of Jesus, we must also claim a measure of reckless passion for our Savior.

Now *that* is radical.

Paul is another prime example of what it means to be a radical. He says, in referring to false apostles,

> I have worked harder, been put in prison more often, been whipped times without number, and faced death again and again. . . . Three times I was beaten with rods. Once I was stoned. Three times I was shipwrecked. Once I spent

a whole night and a day adrift at sea. I have traveled on many long journeys. I have faced danger from rivers and from robbers. I have faced danger from my own people, the Jews, as well as from the Gentiles. I have faced danger in the cities, in the deserts, and on the seas. And I have faced danger from men who claim to be believers but are not. 2 CORINTHIANS 11:23, 25-26

What changes must take place in your life to be a more radical, more contagious Christian? As scary as it may seem, we need to pray that God will give us a clear revelation of who we are and who he desires us to be. And then we need to do whatever it is he calls us to do, no matter how radical it may seem.

Living Out True Religion

One of the biggest hang-ups to living radically for God is religion—or maybe I should say *false* religion. Too often people see religion as a set of rules or a confining box intended to control people. True religion, however, has nothing to do with denomination, worship style, legalism, or how many times you show up at church each week. According to Scripture, "pure and genuine religion in the sight of God the Father means caring for orphans and widows in their distress and refusing to let the world corrupt you" (James 1:27). In other words, true religion involves a complete transformation of the way we think, act, talk, and serve.

If I could take your shoulders right now, look directly into your eyes, and maybe shake you a bit (ever so lovingly, of course!), this is the message I would want to drive home to you: *True religion must not be used to control others. True religion must be used to serve others.*

Let's take a moment to look at another radical disciple of Christ who got this vision of what religion is meant to be: John the Baptist.

> He was in the wilderness and preached that people should
> be baptized to show that they had repented of their sins and
> turned to God to be forgiven. All of Judea, including all the
> people of Jerusalem, went out to see and hear John. And when
> they confessed their sins, he baptized them in the Jordan River.
> His clothes were woven from coarse camel hair, and he wore
> a leather belt around his waist. For food he ate locusts and
> wild honey.
>
> John announced: "Someone is coming soon who is greater
> than I am—so much greater that I'm not even worthy to
> stoop down like a slave and untie the straps of his sandals.
> I baptize you with water, but he will baptize you with the
> Holy Spirit!" MARK 1:4-8

John has no desire to become wrapped up in the religion of his day. He doesn't dress like or look like or act like the religious leaders, who wear robes and sashes intended to reflect their high position in society. John has no desire to impress anyone with his appearance. He cares only about his message. John the Baptist has a clear purpose—to point people to the Messiah. We might not be asked to dress in camel's hair and eat locusts, but our mission is the same as John's. We are called to point people to Christ, no matter the cost.

John most assuredly knows the danger that looms for him as a result of choosing to live as a radical for Christ, but that never stops him from telling the truth of God's Word. After his ministry period in Samaria, John is thrown in prison by Herod after he calls Herod out on the sin in his life that is polluting his entire territory. This gives John some enemies in high places, including Herod's wife. Not long after, at Herod's birthday feast, she requests John's head on a platter . . . and Herod complies (see Matthew 14:8).

John's radicalism costs him his life.

I wonder how many of us are guilty of losing our edge, how many of us have gotten so caught up with life that we have forgotten how to live. Somewhere along the way we have civilized Christianity. Somehow we have started to "play church" and have decided that being a believer has nothing to do with risk or sacrifice. How many of us would be willing to live like Paul or John the Baptist—ready to risk everything, even our own lives, for the call of Christ?

True religion must not be used to control others. True religion must be used to serve others.

Are we willing to take Jesus' words to heart? "Those who love their life in this world will lose it. Those who care nothing for their life in this world will keep it for eternity. Anyone who wants to be my disciple must follow me, because my servants must be where I am. And the Father will honor anyone who serves me" (John 12:25-26).

When you choose to dive into the deep end with Jesus, you will unknowingly find yourself becoming a radical! The more you embrace your purpose, the closer you get to Jesus. The more you know him, the more you trust him. The more you trust him, the more you love him. And the more you love him, the more you love others as well.

Rock On

Okay, I want you to picture being at a rock concert for a moment. I suppose a concert of any kind will suffice, but a rock concert is most applicable. Imagine that you don't know much about the band—you're just going because your friends roped you in. The concert is about to begin, and you are positioned securely in your stadium seat, with no intention of moving (you are more interested in your ice-cold Dr Pepper). And then, without warning, the entire arena goes pitch black. The crowd begins to roar, a faint guitar begins to hum onstage, and a few beams of light begin to dance around the screaming fans. And then, like a jolt from an energy drink, the lights come up, and the music starts blaring as the band takes the stage! The music is so loud that you can't even hear your ice cubes clinking, and your present company is already working up a sweat from all their jumping and screaming.

As the night continues, the band starts growing on you. You start tapping your feet and humming along. You decide that the music is actually pretty good. By the end of the night, your Dr Pepper has long been dropped to the floor and you're acting just as crazy as your friends—jumping around and mouthing the lyrics to songs you've never heard before tonight.

When you first took your seat, you weren't even sure who you were there to see, but as the concert progressed, your adrenaline ramped up, the excitement and energy of the music took over, and you got radical! By the end of the night, you found yourself walking to the car with a new T-shirt displaying the faces of the band members across your back, and of course the complete CD collection. Yep—you are sold out!

For me, knowing God is like being in the presence of a rock

star. It is an adrenaline rush like no other. It is a feeling of liberation that leads me to fulfill the deepest longings of my soul. It leads to an untamed faith that causes my civilized friends to stare at me and gasp. It is all about losing my life for the sake of Christ.

Are you ready to make that commitment today? Are you ready to pursue a new, more radical you? Will you leave your past nailed to the cross and believe that your God is bigger than you ever imagined him to be? Are you willing to embrace your inner daredevil and live a life that is named by God?

> YOU ARE NAMED BY GOD: *You are a radical.*

A Final Word

AS WE WRAP UP OUR TIME TOGETHER, I pray that God will use this journey we've been on for his glory. I hope this time has given you new insights, a deepened appreciation for the Word of God, and fresh gratitude for the grace-filled love of the Lord. How it would thrill my soul to meet you in person, to listen to your stories, to hear about your personal journey and the lessons you've learned along the way. I have no doubt you could teach me a thing or two about endurance, suffering, joy, and love.

As I look back on my life, I am amazed at the thread of God's grace that runs through it. I have fought through the struggles and pain of my past. I have stumbled—and sometimes fallen flat on my face—as God worked to transform my present. And I humbly look ahead to the "immeasurably more" he has in store for my future.

Sometimes I wonder what would have happened if I had just quit—if I'd given up right there in the aftermath of my sin. What if I had waited out the rest of my earthly existence simply going through the motions—attending church, going to small group, volunteering at my kids' school from time to time, watching television with my husband at night before we drift off to sleep, driving my SUV around to ballet and soccer practice—without ever waking up to the reality of who God is and what he wants for my life?

I'll tell you what I would have missed out on:

- a marriage that has faced the fires of hell and has endured to resemble the beautiful reflection of Jesus Christ and his love for his people
- a family that grows each day in our love for one another and our love for God's Word
- a newfound appreciation for the core group of people in my life who have stuck by me and reassured me that I'm not alone
- a fresh perspective with which to see the painful storms of this life
- a new calling to teach and encourage others to love Scripture
- a deep-water adventure with the Lord each day

Are you feeling tempted to quit or remain complacent in your relationship with God right now? Is there something God is calling you to do, but you're making excuses?

God is calling you to move to a new town. *But, God . . .*
God is calling you to a different job. *But, God . . .*
God is calling you to sell some of your treasured possessions. *But, God . . .*

God is calling you to surrender your life to the mission field.
But, God . . .
God is calling you to forgive that person who hurt you.
But, God . . .
God is calling you to get involved in a ministry in your
church. *But, God . . .*
God is calling you to ask that waitress if she knows him
personally. *But, God . . .*

What is the "But, God . . ." in your life right now?

Instead of letting the uncertainties of life stop you or cause you to run in the other direction, allow them to make you more faithful, more daring. Instead of questioning and worrying over every little thing, begin to look at life as an adventure. The more winding and dangerous the path, the more rewarding it can be!

Until we meet someday, my treasured one of the King, I will leave you with these words: there is nothing sweeter in this world than an intimate relationship with Jesus Christ. There is no person, no activity, no place, no high that can begin to compare with the incomprehensible rush of the Savior's love. Trust someone who has gone after many different fixes to find love, security, and purpose. Nothing can compare to my Jesus.

Go after him today, my friend, and don't look back! Pursue him as the greatest love of your life. With each day you embark on this sincere quest for him, your past will seem more distant, your purpose for today will be clearer, and your mission for the future will be more exciting.

The next time you doubt your worth or wonder if your life has meaning, know that God has redeemed you—your past, present, and future are covered with his blood. You, loved one, have been named by God.

You will be given a new name by the LORD's own mouth.

ISAIAH 62:2

Acknowledgments

Thank you does not seem adequate, but I want to extend my thanks to the following people anyway.

To Justin, the man God gave me to marry, love, and do life with. Thank you for your forgiveness, your tenderness, your patience, and your guidance. Thank you for partnering with me to raise two beautiful gifts from God. Thank you for loving on the kids while I write, for praying for me in my storms, and for encouraging me in my times of need. Thank you for loving me with the unconditional love Christ intended. Lord willing, I look forward to those rocking chairs on the back porch and many more years of watching *Lonesome Dove* together.

To my Emma Grace and Lake. You will never know the absolute joy you are to my life. From the moment you were given to me, I have understood more fully the love of the heavenly Father. It is a privilege and an honor to be your mother and to be allowed the opportunity to raise you to have a relationship with your one true Father.

To the woman I aspire to be more like each day—my mother,

Krecia. While on this earth, you were the essence of one who praises in the storm. You have shone your beautiful light into the hearts of so many and will continue to do so through the legacy you have given to us—your children and grandchildren. The battle has been won; the victory is his! Thank you for loving me and showing Christ to me.

To my precious family members, my church family, my KVM team, and the many godly friends who have impacted my life. Aside from the power of Christ, I am the person I am today because of those who have chosen to stand beside me in the most difficult of times. I praise God for friends who have loved me at all times (see Proverbs 17:17) and who have not forsaken me (see Proverbs 27:10).

To my parents, Robert and Cheryl, Randy and Stephanie. Thank you for loving me, supporting me, and praying for me.

To my grandparents, Willard and Juanita. Thank you for believing in me, investing in me, and being the heroes of my life.

To my supernaturally gifted family at Tyndale House Publishers. You are God's immeasurably more in my life, and your belief in what God has put on my heart continues to leave me speechless.

To the many people who have graced the pages of my life story thus far—both the ones I currently share life with and the ones who have just passed through. Thank you for making your mark on my life. Although I have many regrets, there is not one person I regret meeting, knowing, and doing a little life with! Whether our experiences were difficult or joyful at the time, you have been a part of my journey home, and for that I am eternally grateful.

About the Author

Kasey Van Norman is a Bible teacher who is passionate about people and the proclaiming of the gospel. As the founder and president of Kasey Van Norman Ministries, based in College Station, Texas, her heart's desire is to be a fresh voice that bridges the gap between the church and the lost. Kasey's teaching style, whether she's speaking or writing, radiates a refreshing authenticity as she speaks to a generation that is tired of hypocrisy and hungry for transparent leaders. Kasey's ability to relate to others, as well as to promote supernatural bondage breaking, grows out of surviving a lifetime of difficult circumstances. And she didn't simply survive; she was transformed when she came face-to-face with the love and grace of God.

Kasey is married to Justin, her best friend, college sweetheart, and a man who continually models the love and grace of Jesus to her. The couple resides in College Station, Texas. They have two children: Emma Grace and Lake.

You are invited to discover your
true identity by drawing closer
to the one who named you!

Join **Kasey Van Norman** in pursuit of
what it means to be truly *Named by God*!

Named by God: Women of all ages will be able to connect with Kasey as she shares her story of God's infinite grace and compassion. As you journey with Kasey through Scripture and her personal experiences, you'll grow in your relationship with God.

Named by God Bible Study: Join Kasey as she leads you on a six-week journey of transformation! This interactive study will equip you to move beyond past hurts, bring power into your present circumstances, and ignite a victorious faith for your future.

Named by God Leader's Guide: As Kasey shares personal stories and directs you toward a more intimate relationship with Jesus Christ, this leader's guide will equip you to facilitate a life-changing journey through God's Word.

Named by God Video Curriculum: Join Kasey on this life-transforming journey by adding her six-session DVD curriculum to your personal or group study of *Named by God.*

Coming Soon!

Kasey Van Norman Ministries'
Raw Faith Series